RED GOLD

Peak Performance Techniques of the Russian and East German Olympic Victors

GRIGORI RAIPORT, M.D., Ph.D.
(Motivational Psychologist for the USSR Olympic Team)

WITH MONIQUE RAPHAEL HIGH

Published by
JEREMY P. TARCHER, INC.
Los Angeles
Distributed by St. Martin's Press
New York

To Lina Raiport

Library of Congress Cataloging in Publication Data

Raiport, Grigori.
Red gold.

Bibliography.
1. Psychology—Soviet Union. 2. Performance—Psychological aspects. 3. Success. 4. Self-realization.
I. Title.
BF108.S65R35 1987 158'.9 87-10102
ISBN 0-87477-490-X

Jeremy P. Tarcher, Inc.
9110 Sunset Blvd.
Los Angeles, CA 90069

Design by Deborah Daly

Manufactured in the United States of America
10 9 8 7 6 5 4 3 2 1

First Edition

1991

Red Gold

CONTENTS

PART 2: THE SOVIET AUTO-CONDITIONING TRAINING COURSE

ACKNOWLEDGMENTS

I would like to express my warm gratitude to Monique Raphael High, whose unwavering support and encouragement made this book possible, and to my publisher, Jeremy Tarcher, and my editors, Ted Mason and Hank Stine, for their heroic efforts on my behalf.

Foreword

Sibi imperare maximum imperium est.
To conquer oneself is the greatest conquest.
—ROMAN PROVERB

Interest in peak performance has in recent years moved from the athletic fields to the workplace—especially as it relates to the key positions of manager and CEO.

Peak-performance techniques, once the secret province of some professional and Olympic coaches and top Soviet athletes, increasingly are being explored in articles, books, and on television.

From one-minute managers to celebrated pumpers of iron, from the Olympic playing fields, where gold medals are awarded, to the boardrooms of America's largest corporations, where another kind of gold is the reward, the passion for peak performance has become a national priority.

Why? Because America, once the undisputed dominant force in international athletics and business, is now placing an increasingly distant second or worse.

How are we to explain the Soviet and East German superiority as winners in the Olympic Games, while the U.S., with the largest contingent of athletes, now shows up as an also-ran?

And in corporate boardrooms, how are we to explain the consistent edge shown by the Japanese and others in area after area of commerce and industry?

Some might say Americans have lost their clear vision and follow-through, that they now lack the ability to see and stay with a course all the way to its successful outcome.

Certainly I have witnessed this among the readers of my own book, *The One Minute Manager,* and other business best-sellers. It is disquieting to discover how often those who are "in search of excellence" stop part way through a program or book once they feel they have grasped the basics but fail to follow through with the important details. This failure inevitably leads to second place at best.

Now Dr. Grigori Raiport, a former Soviet psychologist who chose to live in the West, gives us the valuable Soviet athletic program in detail and lets us see how we can apply it to our own lives.

Those who read his *Red Gold: Peak Performance Techniques of the Russian and East German Olympic Victors* are best advised to follow his suggestions and work step-by-step through the entire Soviet Auto-Conditioning Training Course.

Only by sticking with this course until the end will you, the reader, be able to gain its full benefit and make the techniques outlined within the covers of this book an integral part of your daily life.

While the author understandably makes much of the Soviet peak-performance techniques, readers need not feel that using these techniques constitutes in any way a political endorsement of the Soviet or community state. As the author himself points out in his Introduction and Afterword, the Soviet system is full of many imperfections that operate to prevent the application of peak performance by the average citizen.

In the West, it would appear far easier for anyone to learn about what few Soviets know—those peak-performance techniques taught to an elite group. Here, we are free to use these in business and in life to achieve extraordinary results.

Therefore the reader is advised to, in the author's words, employ "a compendium of the best aspects" of Soviet peak-performance techniques and Western life. The idea is to use what top Soviet athletes use and to take advantage of all that the Western world has to offer.

Although this book will take more than one minute to read and master, the reader who consistently uses what Dr. Raiport reveals in *Red Gold* can well enjoy a lifetime of personal peak performances.

Spencer Johnson, M.D.
Co-Author, The One Minute Manager

INTRODUCTION

Once again, the Soviet Union and East Germany have taken the gold at the XV Winter Olympics, while the American team came home virtually empty handed. The Soviets won first place with a total of 29 medals (11 gold), while the East Germans breezed into second place with 25 medals (9 gold). The US, on the other hand, came in ninth with only 6 medals (2 gold). Clearly, as in so many previous years, the Soviet bloc athletes earned the lion's share of Olympic gold. What is their secret? To me, the answer is obvious: sports psychology.

This is a book about the theories and techniques of Soviet sports psychology that are used by Russian athletes, chess players, politicians to give them the competitive edge that has earned them an enviable reputation as superachievers. The book is not a comprehensive cataloging of modern Soviet thought or achievement in the field of psychology. Instead, I have focused on one area with which I have had personal experience: performance enhancement, or the field of latent human possibilities, as the Soviets like to call it.

The importance of an athlete's mental state during competition was recognized more than 2,000 years ago in Greece, the cradle of the Olympics. Nowadays, most top athletes understand the paramount role of the mental state in successful performance. Bruce Jenner, the American winner of a gold medal in the decathlon in previous Olympic Games, once said, "Athletic competition is 80 percent mental challenge and 20 percent physical challenge."

Although the importance of the mental challenge is widely recognized, the methods in Soviet sports psychology for meeting this challenge are not well known outside the Soviet sphere of influence. Most of the sports-psychology publications in the USSR are classified as secret, because the mental techniques used in sports psychology are also used in Soviet military and space programs. There is no basic difference between the psychological requirements of an athlete and that of a jet-fighter pilot or cosmonaut.

My knowledge of the peak-performance techniques of Soviet superachievers comes from personal experience. After graduating from medical school in my native city of Rostov, I was selected for advanced studies at the prestigious National Research Institute of Physical Culture in Moscow, where I received a Ph.D. in sports psychology. The National Research Institute is a mighty factory designed to mass-produce Olympic champions like a Detroit assembly line turns out automobiles. It was there that I witnessed "The Big Red Machine" in action.

In essence, the Institute is a laboratory or think tank where the best Soviet minds are challenged to explore the realm of peak performance. The Institute is designed to produce a special breed of psychologist, the sports psychologist. Students are chosen from among the country's top graduates in psychiatry: the sports psychologist must have a clear understanding of the human body from his experience as a medical doctor as well as an understanding of each athlete's psyche.

At the Institute, I worked with several USSR teams (including the Dynamo Soccer Club) and with individual athletes. In 1976 I was one of a handful of psychiatrist/psychologists assigned to the Soviet Olympic team. My patients included gymnast Ludmilla Turischeva and weightlifter Vassili Alexeev.

The Institute's activities are not limited by the boundaries of the USSR. While I was there, I saw large numbers of East German scientists actively collaborating with their Soviet colleagues. Thus, the same techniques and processes are used for training athletes in the USSR and in East Germany. I believe that these techniques have been and will continue to be the major factor in producing "red gold" at the Olympic Games.

Although my experiences at the Institute were invaluable, it was impossible for me to express myself fully as a doctor and thinker in the Soviet Union, where Western psychiatry is shunned and Freud and Jung are on the list of forbidden authors. Shortly after the 1976 Games at Montreal, I had the opportunity to defect.

I arrived in the United States in October 1977, sure that the American public could make use of my knowledge of Soviet peak-performance techniques. I decided to explore the "American way" and to mold my knowledge of Soviet learning techniques to fit Western needs. The result is this book.

I consider myself a psychological hybrid, equipped with knowledge from both sides of the Iron Curtain that enables me to point out how the ideas that originated in Moscow can best be adapted to the Western life-style. The techniques that seem to give the Russians a valuable competitive edge are not so mysterious after all. None of the exercises in this book are difficult—in fact, they are simple enough to be foolproof. They can be beneficial mental tools for anyone.

The ideas and exercises you will find here are a compendium of the best aspects of my own training, both as a staff psychiatrist in the Russian hospital system and later as a sports psychologist.

The techniques I describe can be used successfully by anyone in sports, business, the professions, and many other areas of human endeavor. I hope they enable readers to capture their personal equivalents of gold medals in their own lives.

HOW TO USE THIS BOOK

At the request of my American publisher, I have included exercises at the end of chapters 2 through 8 of this book. These exercises will enable you to put the principles illustrated in each chapter to work in your life immediately. In Part 2 you will find many of these exercises repeated, in somewhat different form, as The Soviet Auto-Conditioning Training Course. My own preference would be for you to undertake the full Auto-Conditioning Training Course. Then, go back to Part 1 and make use of the exercises there that do not appear in Part 2. You will get far more benefit from them after mastering auto-conditioning training.

My strongest advice is to allow a week of practice for each individual exercise. In my experience, this is the minimum time required to achieve proficiency and to master each step.

PART 1

Red Gold

1 THE RUSSIAN EDGE

THE QUEST FOR EXCELLENCE

Russian and East German athletes begin their quest for Olympic gold early. It is part and parcel of the Soviets' unique approach to education and the development of individual talent. In one sense its roots lie in propaganda; in another it is the result of a unique view of and approach to human potential.

In the Soviet Union, the central authority for education is the Moscow-based V. I. Lenin Pedagogical Institute. The Lenin Institute determines the optimal conditions for the education of Soviet superachievers in athletics and other fields, and it instructs the *spetzshkola* (schools for the gifted) in the most advanced methods for developing potential.

How do the Soviets pick out their gifted students? In the United States, the emphasis is on the student's overall achievement in all academic areas. A student with poor math grades, for example, is not likely to gain admittance to a class for the gifted even if her English scores are unusually high, for her overall average is not impressive.

Soviet educators, in contrast, believe that a solid academic average is often merely the expression of good study habits and a fair mind rather than a truly gifted one. They believe that a "jack-of-all-trades" cannot be molded into a master in any single discipline. Instead, Soviet educators look for unexpected brilliance that could be the mark of talent in a specific area. Pupils who show such brilliance are selected for special training.

The procedure works as follows. Every large Russian city has a number of *spetzshkolas*, each of which specializes in training children gifted in a particular field, such as athletics, science, or medicine. Let's say a high school teacher notices that a particular student shows unusual talent in figure skating. The teacher notifies the principal, who transmits a report to the local *spetzshkola* that emphasizes the study of athletics. Then an official from the athletic *spetzshkola* comes to test the youngster. If the student passes a comprehensive screening process, he is sent to the *spetzshkola*, where his athletic talent will be fully developed through the most advanced teaching procedures.

At the *spetzshkola*, students are trained to think and solve problems for themselves through a classical approach all but ignored in the West. For example, in a science *spetzshkola*, the pupils are not taught Newton's laws; rather, they are presented with conditions through which enterprising students can "discover" these laws on their own.

Teaching by rote is rare in the Soviet educational system. Students are bombarded with material, on the assumption that each individual's saturation point for learning is different, and each student's mind will automatically "shut off" on its own when that point is reached. This allows all students to be exposed to all the knowledge they can possibly absorb as quickly as they can absorb it. As a result, primary and secondary education (grammar school through high school) generally takes only ten years. First grade usually begins at age seven, and two general examinations must be passed in the tenth grade: one to receive a high school diploma, and the other to gain admittance to a university. Of course, if a student's area of specialization is physics, his scores in physics and other sciences will be judged far more critically than his scores in literature or philosophy, and vice versa. In the Soviet Union, a high school diploma entitles a student to enter a particular school of study or faculty at the university. Athletics is one such faculty, and it is entered immediately upon finishing high school. One is not required to undergo a program of general studies before beginning advanced specialization, as in the United States, but the length of study is longer in Russia—six years instead of the customary four in American universities—and more rigorous.

Just as the Soviets are constantly on the lookout for specially gifted intellects, they are also searching for specially gifted athletes. The Soviets do not believe in *born* soccer players, or *born* gymnasts. Instead, they believe that gifted young athletes with specific abilities can be directed toward mastery in a particular sport. Those who attend sports *spetzshkolas* engage in a variety of sports before their particular talents are guided toward specific areas.

Authorities look for youngsters with a good general mastery of sports skills, along with the right blend of psychological characteristics: competitiveness, perseverance, and high resistance to pain. If, after being exposed to various sports, a child appears to demonstrate a social orientation, the school coaches will direct him toward a team sport; if the child shows a more solitary nature, he will be directed toward sports that stress the individual's skills, such as running, boxing, or gymnastics.

The sports *spetzshkola* molds the youngster's raw capabilities to fit the requirements of the sport to which his particular abilities predispose him, although he will have many opportunities to test his skills in a variety of suitable sports before a final selection is made.

BIRTH OF ATHLETIC SUPERIORITY IN THE USSR

Outside the walls of the Moscow Research Institute of Physical Culture, most Soviet citizens know little about the field of sports psychology. Because its methods are also used in the space and defense programs, it is surrounded by an official wall of secrecy. Many publications are classified and distributed only among a close-knit clan of specialists. In fact, the Committee for Physical Culture and Sports—the highest organ regulating all athletic activities in the USSR—is not an adjunct of any ministry, such as that of health or education, but belongs to the Department of Propaganda itself. In other words, the main function of sports in the Soviet Union is not to promote health or international détente, but to promote the Communist way of life.

Like so many other things, sports shares a dual function in Soviet affairs: its internal role is military related; its external role is that of propaganda, showing the world the superiority of Soviet society. To fulfill these goals, the state spends billions of dollars. A cabinet-level Department of Sports, and the Committee for Physical Culture and

Sports, dispense these funds according to carefully laid long-term plans. The five-year plan for the period 1980–1985 was to build in the USSR 725 swimming pools, 9,800 soccer fields, more than 500 stadiums, 10,000 gymnasiums, and 3,000 track-and-field arenas.

As far as the military aspects of Soviet athletic training go, every athlete is expected to be a potential crack soldier. Needless to say, when a nation mobilizes its total mental and physical resources for war (or any other endeavor) it gains a significant edge over prospective opponents who have not done so. Each physically capable Soviet citizen (female as well as male) must undergo a rather unpopular sports test called GTO (*Gotov K Trudu i Oborone*), Ready for Defense. The military aspect of sports training accounts for the strength of its appeal throughout the USSR, where 82 million Soviet citizens belong to 230,000 sports clubs. War is not looked upon as merely a possibility, but as an inevitable reality demanding constant readiness.

The propaganda aspects of the Soviet drive for athletic excellence began in the early 1920s with a search for techniques that would ensure victory in the 1924 Olympic Games and "prove" the innate superiority of the Communist system over all others. These Games were the first in which post-tsarist Russia would be competing. It was, therefore, a supreme opportunity for the young Soviet government to prove itself to the outside world and to display the superiority of its system through the performance of its athletes.

Soviet psychology, in pursuit of practical results, now concentrated on a strategic task: maximizing human performance for the glory of the USSR. With this goal in mind, Leningrad's Professor Alexander Puni became the country's first sports psychologist in 1924, seeking ways to elicit the best performance from the finest Soviet athletes. The Soviets consider their ability to produce top scientists, cosmonauts, diplomats, soldiers, dancers, and athletes as a reflection of the nation as a whole, a demonstration to the world that the Communist government in no way hampers personal brilliance.

In order to determine the outer limits of human potential, the primary task at the Moscow Research Institute of Physical Culture is to define the human being, concentrating on the three essential areas of human nature: the physical, the mental, and the emotional. Researchers at the Institute then attempt to develop techniques to push the individual to fulfill his or her maximum potential—in other words, to achieve peak performance. Attaining peak performance, or state of optimal functioning, is what sets winners apart from losers.

THE PSYCHOLOGY OF VICTORY

Most Soviet sports psychologists are trained, as I was, at the Moscow Research Institute of Physical Culture. The Institute is set within a group of guarded buildings that house the utmost in sophisticated sports-training equipment. Its faculty consists of the nation's most highly trained specialists, whose expertise ranges from biochemistry to psychoneurology. Because the state and its leaders expect better and longer-lasting winners at every international competition, the Institute functions in a constant state of urgency.

The Institute, under the directive of the Committee

for Physical Culture and Sports, also operates an impressive intelligence network: gathering data on foreign athletes (especially in the West), purchasing the newest foreign books, observing Western athletic clubs and locker rooms and reporting on any new sports secrets that are learned. Western methods, though not officially promoted in the USSR, nevertheless find their way into Soviet training labs and research.

The Institute is really an elite think tank concerned with the single objective of creating winners. The graduate students in sports psychology are medical doctors trained in psychiatry. For, in order to produce winning athletes, sports psychologists have to understand the three realms that comprise a human being: the body, the emotions, and the mind. The Institute's objective is to explore that special state of inspiration in which a particular human being can surmount great obstacles, and then to learn to teach athletes and coaches how to re-create this state at will.

My own interests inclined me toward the most exciting field of Soviet psychology, the tapping of human potential—and in the USSR, that means becoming a sports psychologist. For one thing, I was an athlete myself, a boxer, and had always wondered: What were the forces affecting athletic performance?

I had witnessed on more than a few occasions the seemingly inexplicable phenomenon of a weaker, smaller opponent's decimation of an obviously stronger challenger. What was the magic behind such a feat? I myself had felt this special sort of glory come over me on occasion, always at times when no one was able to stop me in the ring. At other times, a mysterious cloak of ineptitude descended, causing me to move clumsily on heavy feet, vulnerable and already defeated before I could deliver my first punch.

This led me to suspect that vast, untapped reserves of strength are available to all of us as human beings, that we are capable of far greater achievements than we habitually produce, that somehow our real mental powers are barred by invisible forces keeping us chained to mediocrity. I felt certain that lying within each of us was the capacity to be much smarter, much kinder, and much better able to overcome the petty conflicts and frictions that mar our lives. I firmly believed that sports psychology held out the rare opportunity to enhance the performance not only of normal individuals but also of athletes.

During my training, I was exposed to every technique available in the area of sports psychology, among them: auto-conditioning training, psychoregulation, and ideomotor training. I soon realized that all of these methods could just as practically be applied to other fields in which human beings exerted their creativity. If a gymnast such as Ludmilla Turischeva could learn to psych herself up before a performance, why not a violinist or an actor? Why not a businessman before an important board meeting, or a surgeon before a crucial operation?

Indeed, the thought struck me that *every human being, at some point, has undergone this special state of optimal functioning*—this moment of clarity when all goals suddenly appear attainable, when one feels oneself invincible and full of power. I stored this idea away. Someday, somehow, I would find a way to spread my knowledge to a broader spectrum of society, so that athletes would not be the sole recipients to benefit from the techniques I had learned in Moscow.

As a graduate student working at the Institute, my other duties included trying to match young athletes, age six to nine, to the sport most appropriate to their aptitudes. It's not enough for little Boris to want to be a basketball player, if his neurological apparatus is better suited to gymnastics or weightlifting.

It was my job to put children through a battery of psychophysiological tests designed to determine which particular form of athletic endeavor suited them best. These tests included measurements of reaction time, muscle response, type of muscular tissue, and duration and strength of attention. This process was thought to save children years of disappointment that might have resulted if they had focused on a sport to which they were not constitutionally or psychologically fitted. For instance, one of the most important characteristics required for weightlifting is explosiveness—the ability to exert tremendous amounts of energy within a very short period of time. A marathon runner's most important trait, on the other hand, is endurance—the ability to sustain exertion for prolonged periods. By testing a young athlete's nervous system, we determined his particular strengths and guided the child toward an appropriate sport. Of course, our recommendations were not compulsory; parents were at liberty to consider them or brush them off.

To give you some idea of the scope of sports psychology in the Soviet Union, my job posed the following challenges: to rid an athlete of stress and train him instead to pass this stress on to an opponent; to forecast an athlete's performance; to "psych up" members of our team and "psych out" rivals; to teach our athletes how to gain control over emotions and thoughts; and, finally, to help them enhance their natural personality traits by teaching them to become more assertive, competitive, and self-disciplined.

As an American reader, you may find that some of the ideas presented in this book make you feel uncomfortable, for they will challenge your habitual beliefs. I urge you not to reject them outright, but at least to consider the information presented. The reward for your intellectual tolerance will be acquisition of some practical techniques to expedite your own personal development.

Everyone, not just athletes, can benefit from the results. In a capsule, the idea is to get to know who you are and what abilities you possess. With this knowledge, you will be free to go ahead and fulfill all your potentials.

In the remainder of this book, we will discuss the Soviet techniques of performance enhancement that give East German and Russian athletes their edge, and show how the Western individual can make use of them. We will concentrate on the three areas dealt with at the Moscow Institute: the physical, mental, and emotional. For, to become the best person we each can be, we must view our self as a composite being with different facets, each of which deserves to achieve its own "personal best."

2 CONQUERING YOUR RESISTANCE TO CHANGE

In training athletes in the techniques of peak performance, Soviet sports psychologists have discovered that the first problem they have to deal with is the human organism's natural resistance to change.

Soviet psychologists specializing in peak performance techniques (almost exclusively sports psychologists, although their clients may include others besides athletes) believe that to become a true winner, athletes must develop their personalities as well as their bodies. These psychologists point to numerous examples of victors who were less gifted or well endowed than their adversaries but triumphed through sheer power of personality or will. Therefore, the concept of personality development is a cornerstone of Russian theory and practice in the field of performance enhancement.

According to Soviet theory, we all possess enormous possibilities inherent in our nervous system and brain. The axons (the neuron's tentacles conducting electrical impulses) are capable of creating infinite combinations of neuron chains and, therefore, infinite human possibilities.

But Soviet psychologists see these possibilities as just that, nothing more. To them, possibilities by definition have no actual existence of their own but must be brought forth, the way the artist's vision of a sculpture must be brought forth from the rock and molded by a conscious act of will in order to become an actuality. In the same manner, Russian performance psychologists are convinced that it is up to each individual to consciously pick up the reins of his or her own development.

In the Soviet view, the goal of peak-performance training is to realize one's perceived as well as one's hidden talents, learning to summon them forth at will by developing the more desirable of the nervous system's infinite possibilities in the attaining of objectives and the achievement of ambitions.

Of course, we all possess an intrinsic drive to excel, to expand the scope of our awareness, to explore new horizons. Why else do human beings constantly seek to break through barriers and explore new, uncharted areas in their lives or in the world? The need to set records, to challenge inner as well as outer boundaries, is as much a part of the human experience as forming governments and structuring languages.

However, the decision to take charge of one's own creation is frightening, for it implies taking responsibility for one's future. Then, too, the process of change is often irreversible and permanent. And there is no one else to blame in case of failure.

FEAR OF CHANGE

In teaching Soviet athletes to develop their personalities in the service of enhanced performance and a greater competitive edge, sports psychologists at Moscow's Research

Institute of Physical Culture found that the most fundamental obstacle they had to overcome was the innate fear of and resistance to change.

The first step toward self-transformation and performance enhancement then, is overcoming the fear of change. This fear usually takes one of three forms:

FEAR OF THE UNKNOWN. This is the fear that must have possessed Aladdin while he was pondering whether to open the bottle to let the genie loose. Most of us are afraid of the powerful giant sleeping in the depths of our psyche. Yet we feel compelled to awaken him and make him work for us, even though we fear what his power might do if we cannot control him.

FEAR OF LOSING IDENTITY. A person cannot live without a sense of self, without knowing who he or she is. A journey of self-transformation implies leaving behind the old self on the road to acquiring a new one. Thus, for the duration of the transformation process we have no real identity. Burning off those mental warts (laziness, insecurity, procrastination) can be quite painful, for we protect our flaws under a sort of "diplomatic immunity" since they are part of our identity. Giving up the old self means essentially choosing a different self around which to construct one's life. Your greatest fear is bound to be that if you cast aside the old you, you may be throwing out your very identity along with it!

FEAR OF SUFFERING. Expanded awareness will make you conscious of your negative traits, bringing embarrassment, loss of self-esteem, and mental pain. Plato, who compared unenlightened people to prisoners in a dark cave, says:

"At first, when any of them is liberated and compelled suddenly to stand up and turn his neck around and walk towards the lights, he will suffer sharp pains; the glare will distress him."

All three of these fears have a single cause, the inherent conservatism of the same human nervous system that paradoxically contains all those infinite possibilities we are trying to bring forth.

HOMEOSTASIS

Conservatism is a universal phenomenon concerned with the preservation of established conditions, resisting any alteration of the status quo. Every living organism possesses some amount of conservatism, necessary for its survival. The physiological basis of conservatism is *homeostasis,* a complex biochemical mechanism designed to fight any deviation from the preexisting state and return the living system to equilibrium.

The mechanisms of homeostasis strive to maintain the constancy of such vital parameters of the body as temperature, blood pressure, pulse rate, and amount of blood sugar. One can't help coming to the conclusion that the human organism is conservative; the strategic task of its physiological mechanisms is to resist change at any cost, preserving the status quo.

It seems logical, therefore, to assume that the part of the nervous system assigned to maintain bodily functions—instincts and natural drives—is conservative as well. Instincts operate on the pleasure principle. The strategic goal of the pleasure principle is to avoid pain, which is caused by a distortion of the initial equilibrium, and to seek pleasure, which is accompanied by a restoration of that equilibrium. Take thirst, for instance. Reduction of the water level in the body causes displeasure, psychologically perceived as thirst. This feeling triggers "water-searching" behavior. Thirst is alleviated by finding and consuming something to drink, which brings on pleasure.

The very nature of instincts—the preservation of existing modes of operation—makes them a primary source of conservatism. Animals, whose behavior is almost entirely ruled by their natural drives, are the embodiment of conservatism. A bird or a bee cannot change its genetically predisposed behavior, and therefore it is predestined to rigid, mechanized activities. It has neither the desire nor the capacity to rationalize its behavior or to choose novel actions. Needless to say, a worker bee couldn't even dream of transforming itself into a queen bee; freedom to choose one's fate is a purely human prerogative.

THE CHANGE EQUATION

With a strong force like homeostasis holding them back, how do human beings manage to change at all? Soviet psychologists have devised a simple equation that they think provides the answer. This equation can be expressed as *SS over SC equals Change*, where *SS* stands for the strength of the stimulus and *SC* for the strength of our conservatism:

$$\textit{Change} = \frac{\textit{Strength of Stimulus}}{\textit{Strength of Conservatism}}$$

In other words, in the Russian view, the intensity of human change depends on two major factors: the strength of the change-producing stimulus, and the strength of the change-resisting forces that comprise the organism's inherent conservatism.

When the strength of the stimulus is great enough, Soviet psychologists believe a quantum leap can be made, resulting in the achievement of previously unrealized potential and performance. According to their theory, two kinds of factors effect change in the human personality: forces from outside the organism; and forces, either physiological or psychological, that arise from within.

It seems there is a correlation between external and internal changes. Whether an event is mental, physical, or emotional, and whether it represents a tragedy or a tremendous improvement in one's life-style (such as getting married or obtaining a much-desired promotion), the mere presence of a strong stimulus can cause a deep psychological transformation.

It is not so much the objective strength of a stimulus that changes us, however, but our subjective responses to it. If we don't allow ourselves to feel the impact of an event deeply, it will just glance off of us without leaving any profound trace. If we perceive the event only on the rational level, not emotionally, it is unlikely to penetrate the depths of our being. It appears that we must have a certain predisposition to embrace change, some kind of inner openness that welcomes novelty, or we will remain essentially the same.

INTERNAL FACTORS. These are more difficult to detect and analyze than external ones. One of the common reasons for seeking change may be sheer boredom. You become aware that you have exhausted—sucked dry—your present mode of existence. You have already tried all experiences available on your current plane of being, and now you are simply bored. You start looking for a new leap upward. Often, such internal cravings for change are too weak to trigger major transformations. Then we need an external push.

EXTERNAL FACTORS. Any strong stimulus possesses the energy to challenge mental homeostasis, thereby causing a personality change. It can be anything—changing a job, an apartment, or a mate. An inner shift may occur as a result of serious illness, a trip abroad, bankruptcy, an encounter with a new philosophy—any event, in short, capable of derailing the train of habitual ways of thinking and feeling. An emergency situation, when our very existence is put into question, often has the most profound effect on us.

The Case of Yosif V.

My friend Yosif V. provides an ideal, if extreme, example of someone in whom both inner and outer stimuli came together to produce a profound change that took him from the heights in one field to equal acclaim in another. Yosif was an Olympic pole-vaulting star who harbored a secret desire to be a boxer. One day during a drunken fight in a bar, Yosif was severely beaten by one of Russia's greatest boxing champions. This devastating experience catalyzed Yosif's determination to change careers and become a championship boxer—and to best the man who had beaten him so humiliatingly.

To his wife's dismay, Yosif abandoned a career that had given them a life-style of material comfort and rewards available in the Soviet Union only to successful politicians, athletes, scientists, and a handful of others who are perceived as significantly advancing the image of the Soviet system. Although she begged him to abandon what to her seemed a foolish idea, Yosif's determination to develop his potential as a boxer had become the dominant force in his life, pushing the warnings of his wife and friends, not to mention the natural human resistance to change, into the background.

My Western friends are always surprised to learn that the one group that did not object to Yosif's change of career was the Soviet state. Soviet authorities tend to view a desire for career change as less dramatic than it is viewed in the United States and other Western countries. The reason for this attitude is simple: Under the Communist system, people are not expected to work for the increase of their own wealth, or even for their own fulfillment. Instead, they are expected to labor for the greater glory and advancement of the Soviet state. The authorities reason that a person who is dissatisfied with his or her work is likely to be less productive; one who is satisfied is likely to give and achieve more.

This is one instance where the Communist system, which in so many other ways represses the individual, works to further personal aspirations. In Yosif's case, the change paid off. He became one of the Soviet Union's most renowned boxers—and eventually won a championship fight against the boxer who had delivered the beating that had set Yosif on the path of personal development and change.

BEGINNING THE PROCESS OF SELF-CHANGE

If you wish to initiate your own process of self-change and start developing some of your own infinite possibilities, it is only logical to begin by outlining what it is you want to accomplish. This is true whether you have a specific goal—such as increasing your proficiency in sports, gaining an edge on a business competitor, or becoming a more gregarious person—or whether you wish merely to make a general improvement in the kind of person you are. Without an objective in mind, self-development can become a blind, uncertain course that leads nowhere.

A popular Russian psychologist, L. E. Ruvinsky, says, "It's difficult to imagine a person living without any goal at all. Everybody has some goal, be it material possessions, entertainment, or pleasure. The more meaningful the goals, . . . the greater is a man. If you get too engulfed by trivial things, you can lose your ability to accomplish big ones."

This idea is echoed by Tolstoy: "Have a goal for the whole life, have a goal for a certain epoch in your life, goal for the year, for a week, for a day, for an hour, for a minute, always keeping in mind your priorities, sacrificing lower goals for the higher ones."

However, Soviet philosophy also holds that the goals you choose must be realistic, accomplishable ones. In his book *Self-Development*, Dr. Ruvinsky argues with the popular Western belief that individual potential is unlimited and therefore anyone can reach any goal. "No, it is simply not true," he states flatly. "How about the Soviet contra-argument: 'Your potential is limited; therefore, choose a realistic goal.' "

"Most things have limitations," writes Ruvinsky. Human longevity, for instance, is limited, but most of us act as if we were going to live forever. An average human lifespan, seventy-two years, is equal to about 26,000 days. "There are definite limits to one's physical strength," continues Ruvinsky, "to one's talent or patience."

As children, we are not aware of any limits. We are born with naive ignorance about our limitations, and only during maturation do we gradually discover them. Children strive to test the possibilities: How many glasses of milk can I drink at a time before I throw up? How fast can I run before getting exhausted? How loudly can I scream?

It is a sign of maturity to know your limits. If you don't, you may be in danger of trying, as the song goes, "to reach the unreachable star." I have seen too many victims of the popular fallacy that you can be whatever you choose to be. I know of no other maxim that has caused as many disappointments.

I assure you, I am a strong adherent of hope. Why else would I have left Russia if not in the hope of finding a more fulfilling life in the West? Yet the Soviets' view of limitations does have merit. It is *unrealistic* hope they oppose. Russian psychologists believe in looking at yourself honestly, and this means being aware of your limitations. Self-definition means setting boundaries around the object you are defining. Knowing *who you are* inevitably implies knowing *what you are not*.

Soviet psychologists believe that self-knowledge is crucial for self-development. Dr. Vladimir Levy, the Soviet authority in the field, maintains, "You cannot change yourself without trying to learn about yourself." On the other hand, he continues, "You cannot learn about yourself without trying to change yourself." And, he concludes, "You can learn about yourself only through actions."

One of America's most popular myths was succinctly formulated by the Success Motivation Institute, a huge Texas corporation. Its motto is: "Whatever you ardently desire . . . will inevitably come true." Yet desire is obviously not enough. Without the ability to realize one's ambition, desire is impotent, a source of frustration. Soviets believe that the opposite of hope is not despair but a realistic assessment of potential.

A proper synthesis of these two extremes, necessity and possibility, results in freedom. As the philosopher Kierkegaard puts it:

> To live only in necessity is to live as if *I am what I am* and can be no different. To live only in possibility is to live as if *I can be whatever I imagine*. Life's greatest tragedies are to be found in people who have carried too much (or too little), who have imagined too much (or too little), or who have willed too much (or too little).

It takes inner strength and wisdom to recognize and accept your own limitations, but only by going through this process will you become able to transcend them.

EXERCISES

Creating a Target-Self

The first step in any practical course of self-development is to become clearly aware of the person you would like to be. Begin by defining your Ideal-Self. Take a pencil and write down all the psychological qualities you would like to acquire or enhance. Try to be as specific and honest as possible. It is important to know what ideals you are striving for.

Once you have formed an image of your Ideal-Self, become aware of the fact that it is not reachable. Ideals, by definition, are not reachable. Webster's Dictionary defines the word *ideal* as "a perfect model, . . . existing only in the mind as an image, fancy. . . ."

Failure to understand the unattainability of an ideal is one of our greatest sources of frustration. A compelling desire to reach the state of perfection defeats the very process of self-development. This desire is the cradle of failure, and the perfectionist is always doomed to fail to achieve his goals.

Disappointment in reaching an ideal can throw us into the opposite direction—rejecting all ideals. A cynic is often a disappointed romantic. As Nietzsche writes:

> Alas, I knew noble men who lost their highest hope. Then they slandered all high hopes. . . . The wings of their spirit broke: and now their spirit crawls about and soils what it gnaws. Once they thought of becoming heroes: now they are voluptuaries. The hero is for them an offense and a fright. . . .Whoever does not know how to find the way to *his* ideal lives more frivolously and impudently than the man without an ideal.

Since your Ideal-Self list cannot serve as a practical model for your self-development, start a new outline. Let's call the new list your Target-Self. This model of your future development will be more realistic and authentic, more congruent with your existing capacities than your Ideal-Self. Don't make your Target-Self too rigid; be ready to modify it as your values and standards keep changing.

Next, under the heading Present-Self, write down those traits or habits that you would like to rid yourself of.

Increasing Your Motivation to Change

Now, let's make use of the Target-Self and Present-Self lists to boost your motivation for self-development. I call this exercise "The Carrot and the Stick":

THE CARROT: Increase your desire to reach your Target-Self (attracting forces).

THE STICK: Increase your dissatisfaction with your Present-Self (repelling forces).

This double pressure will make your quantum leap—from what you are to what you can be—much easier and faster.

It probably will work better if you look at your Present-Self (Stick) first and then consider what your Target-Self (Carrot) might be. Let's say you have decided to get rid of your dull and inefficient Present-Self. Start fostering repelling forces by concentrating on your negative characteristics (lack of self-confidence, indecisiveness, cowardice, etc.). Be as honest as possible, for in this case, the worse the better.

Now, start building up attractive forces. Start picturing all the desirable qualities you want to have (assertiveness, courage, etc.). After you become disgusted enough with your Present-Self, decide on a day to mark the beginning of your ascendance toward your Target-Self, the image of which you have been fostering all this time.

Reserve special times to exercise a desirable quality. For example, if you are lacking assertiveness, say to yourself: "For the next two hours I will act and feel assertive." (Needless to say, it's better to do this exercise around people who are perceptive enough not to misinterpret your assertiveness as aggressiveness or militancy.) In the same way, if you want to become more spontaneous, choose the least threatening situation and just start acting on impulse: be foolish, freely vocalizing your thoughts and feelings.

Keep in mind that the growth of your psychological qualities occurs in the same way as the growth of your muscles. Every time you exercise your biceps, they grow in mass and strength. The same goes for mental functions—courage, for example. Every time you exercise it (every time you act out of courage), your courage grows stronger. You gain confidence in your ability to face situations bravely.

Unlike a caterpillar, whose growth takes place in a protective cocoon, we are rarely afforded the luxury of hiding while we change and develop. The ideal conditions for growth would be to disappear for some time, to choose a new environment and new friends who would accept and support our ascendance to our Target-Self. This is what some Japanese artists do after reaching a plateau in their craft: they move to a different city, changing their name and the style of their painting.

However, if you work consistently at developing your most desirable qualities, you will soon find yourself progressing rapidly, no matter what the opposition. As simple as this process sounds, it will effect a fundamental change in your life. Even more important, it will develop in you a flexibility toward change, a vital step in making use of the Soviet peak-performance techniques that follow.

3 TRANSCENDING YOUR THRESHOLD OF PAIN

Soviet psychologists are convinced that there is no gain without pain, and that it is the fear of pain that holds many people back from achieving their peak performance.

The Soviets believe that all great human achievement is based on overcoming the pleasure principle, thereby breaking away from the dictates of instinct. It is the human element of our psyche—consciousness—that is the source of personal progress, providing us with freedom of choice. To be free *from* something implies to be free *for* something.

Russian psychologists, oriented toward the philosophy of stoicism, recognize the value of pain, often quoting in their writings Albert Einstein: "I have never looked upon ease and happiness as ends in themselves—such ethical basis I call more proper for a herd of swine."

THE VALUE OF PAIN

Soviet psychology postulates the following functions of pain:

INFORMATIVE FUNCTION. Pain never exists without a cause; it is always a symptom of some physical or mental disorder. Thus, a migraine headache may be the symptom of mental tension. But the sufferer, instead of searching for the true cause of the problem (the stress-producing factor) in order to eradicate it, hastily grabs aspirin to dull the symptom (pain).

The Soviets seem uninterested in cause or remedy. Instead, they appear to encourage people to face the pain, to push the limits of human endurance, believing that any substance that will make things easier could lead to addiction. Sleeping pills are rarely used in the USSR, and dentists seldom employ novocaine or nitrous oxide in their routines. Unlike in the West, where hundreds of "designer" as well as standard drugs are available, both through prescriptions and on the black market, in Russia few analgesics are prescribed to alleviate anything but the most severe pain.

DEVELOPMENTAL FUNCTION. In general, displeasure often serves as a motivational force, stimulating activity leading to its elimination. Dissatisfaction with your job, or city, or mate will stimulate you to search for a better one. Thus, pain provides the catalyst to initiate change; in this respect it appears as a progressive force. On the other hand, pleasure is conservative: it seeks continuation, preservation, of the status quo, hence fixating you in stability.

Aristotle noted that "happiness we always desire for its own sake and never as a means to something else."

Therefore, absolute contentment would lead to absolute passivity and stagnation. Indeed, if all your needs were completely satisfied, you would have no motive to alter your state; you would be doomed to dwell in passivity until the whip of dissatisfaction forced you to act once more.

We can see the same mechanism at work behind the glorious progress of the human species. The very complexity of our nervous system is the result of the evolutionary process stimulated by a general motive—optimal avoidance of displeasure. Thus, Homo sapiens is the son of pain, not of pleasure. Dostoyevski was probably right in his conclusion that "suffering is the only cause of consciousness."

Many geniuses credit their sufferings with having elevated them to the heights of their achievement. "Do I not owe to it [illness] infinitely more than to my health?" exclaims Nietzsche, whose ideas are beloved by the Soviet intelligentsia. "I do indeed owe to it a higher kind of health; I owe to it my philosophy. Great pain is a great deliverer." Even Charles Darwin gave due credit to his infirmities: "If I had not been so great an invalid, I should not have done so much."

In the West, most people are reared with the idea that pain is something to be avoided at all cost. Aversion to pain has been imbued in them by their parents' unlimited (and therefore blind) love for them. Someone who is insulated from the thorns of life by overprotective parents remains like a fragile plant cultivated in the controlled atmosphere of a hothouse. Sooner or later, when the protective glass is removed, the plant is easily broken by the harsh winds of real life.

DOLOROPHOBIA

The Soviets maintain that American society tends to promote unlimited hedonism, that advertising and the media place the highest value on a life of luxury, comfort, and fun. Pain is treated as something absolutely negative, even abnormal, that must be eliminated at any price as quickly as possible. As a result, Russians mockingly note, America is becoming a nation of pill-grabbers and hypochondriacs, reacting fearfully to any sign of physical pain or discomfort.

This picture does point out a problem that can cripple human development. When an instant remedy seems to be provided—even encouraged—for every minor ache or malaise, human beings can easily overlook the fact that pain can be a springboard for transformation and development. This is an operative principle of Soviet psychology, applied especially in sports but believed to be applicable in the emotional arena as well.

A tendency to avoid pain at any cost can be considered a special pathology, which I call *dolorophobia*—fear of pain.

NIKITIN'S CHILDREN

One of the goals of Soviet child-rearing efforts is the development of tolerance to pain. Psychologists believe that exposing a child to reasonable obstacles develops his willpower and perseverance, qualities highly valued in the

USSR. This attitude is supported by laboratory experiments with animals. Dr. N. Boyko in the Kiev University lab administered mild electric shocks to baby rats. He discovered that these rats were developing faster than the control (unshocked) group and, as adults, became more confident and less fearful than their more contented peers. The process resembles immunization: small doses of virulent substances increase resistance to real dangers later in life.

A similar experimental method is being applied to young children throughout the Soviet Union. Having remained in close contact with a number of my friends from medical school and from the Institute of Physical Culture, I have been kept apprised of new Soviet theories and methods in the field of child development. Boris Pavlovitch Nikitin, an engineer whose reputation as a pioneer educator has spread throughout the country, might be termed the Soviet Dr. Spock. So-called family clubs have sprouted all over Russia to implement the methods prescribed by Nikitin and tested on his own remarkable offspring. The results have much to teach us about the developmental value of pain.

Nikitin's children have progressed through the school system full speed ahead, having been taught at home and presented with learning tools at a very early age (they began to read at two and a half and were exposed to chemistry at age eight). In terms of physical fitness, they have shown far greater endurance than other children their age. Nikitin's system has something in common with that of the ancient Mongols, for his children were running barefoot through snow and swimming in ice-cold lakes and rivers almost from infancy. As a result, they hardly ever fell prey to colds and flu. They were brought up to be afraid of almost nothing and to overcome all obstacles as a matter of course. The family clubs engendered by the Nikitin methods have turned out hardier, less fearful youngsters, proving the veracity of Nikitin's notion that most children can develop into mental and physical winners if they are given the correct motivation, encouragement, and tools and are allowed to come into natural, unimpeded contact with the elements, including pain.

The popularity of the Nikitin system is not surprising in a country where the maxium "Love your suffering" seems to be a way of life for many athletes. Sports champions proved the theory that pain is the bridge to success. Nowhere is this concept emphasized as rigorously as in the Soviet Union. While working in Moscow with weightlifters, I often heard their testimony that "the muscle starts really growing when it starts hurting." When I worked with dancers from the Bolshoi ballet company, I remember the sense of accomplishment they would feel once they had passed through the barrier of tolerance to pain. They felt that they had outdone themselves in the fiercest competition of all: against their own previous record.

Ludmilla Turischeva, the champion Soviet gymnast, used to practice at the bar until her body literally rebelled and she could not continue. Each day, I would put her in the auto-conditioning state (see Chapter 6 exercises and Part 2) and teach her how to use her pain as an ally rather than an enemy. By learning to accept pain, she learned to tolerate it longer and accomplished more.

To generalize this experience, we can postulate that change and growth mostly occur upon reaching and exceeding your threshold of pain.

THRESHOLD OF PAIN (TOP)

Let's suppose that in the gym you usually push eighty pounds ten times. You have tried to push a heavier weight but it hurt, so you decided to stay with eighty pounds. Performing this routine regularly will keep your muscle tone at a certain level, but it will not increase either the mass of your muscles or their strength. If you want to break the equilibrium and conquer new heights of strength, you must exceed your TOP.

This rule is applicable for development of one's mental functions as well. Every one of them—courage, patience, intellect—has its own threshold. It is important to know your TOPs for various functions. Often the mere awareness of these TOPs enables you to transcend them.

I had an interesting patient in Moscow named Alla, a marathon runner whose endurance was inconsistent. After I got to know her, I began to notice some interesting parallels between her running and her temper. Alla was usually quite calm and reasonable, but sometimes she would burst into almost hysterical rage, exploding into a kind of animal shrieking that surprised even her with its overpowering violence. I noticed that this rage was usually brought on by emotional exhaustion when she had to quit a race suddenly, her heart palpitating and body aching.

"Clearly," I said to her, "you've never learned to cross your TOPs, either physical or emotional. Let's first look at your running. Learn to become aware of the moment when you first feel your body giving out from the exercise. Appreciate how tired you are, and then slow down and start to breathe more slowly. Mentally detach yourself from your body and watch your feet continuing to run.

In about thirty seconds you will be surprised to find that you have passed beyond your TOP, and your pride in this accomplishment will manifest itself in every limb of your body."

I gave Alla similar advice about her apparently unconquerable rages. "The next time your husband or child goads you into an argument, hold yourself back by separating yourself from your anger. Look at yourself from an outside perspective, and start to breathe slowly and deeply. In a moment, you will have crossed your emotional TOP. And as it happens your heart will fill with pride, and you'll be able to deal with your husband's or your son's demands in a rational, measured fashion."

To my satisfaction, Alla's ability to run marathons improved within weeks, and her family reported that her temper tantrums declined in frequency in about the same time.

You will appreciate the significance of TOP more if you consider an alternative meaning for it—threshold of performance.

EXERCISE

Raising Your Threshold of Pain

It is relatively easy to find your TOPs. This is how to do it:

- To find the TOP of your courage, recall the time in your life when you were most afraid.
- The same goes for your patience. Recall a situation in which you most completely lost your patience.
- Conduct a similar inventory for your other psychological traits: assertiveness, competitiveness, perseverance, etc.
- Once you know your limits, you can start exceeding them. Start establishing a PR (personal record) for each quality that you would like to improve. For example, if you discover that your threshold of patience is limited to one hour of uninterrupted reading at one sitting, set yourself a goal to endure a whole hour and a half tonight. If your desire to lose weight is overwhelmed by a constant need to eat snacks, learn to raise your threshold of hunger by forcing yourself to endure its pangs for half an hour longer than you used to. It is a known fact in Russia that once people exceed their habitual limits, they begin to achieve heightened levels of performance. And heightened levels of performance are what the quest for the Russian edge is all about.

4 MASTERING CONSCIOUSNESS AND ATTENTION

According to Soviet psychological theory, learn to control your attention and you learn to control your destiny.

In the Soviet Union, the goal of self-development and performance training is to teach people to choose perceptions of reality that will allow them to determine their own states of consciousness. The idea is that a person independent of outside stimuli can select which stimuli will affect his or her perceptions. Russian psychologists have developed this art to a high degree, and it is used by Soviet citizens to gain an extraordinary amount of control over their reactions and performance.

For millennia, the phenomenon of consciousness has been the subject of heated debates among various philosophical schools and religious doctrines. Founders of Western psychology have not always agreed on the nature of consciousness, some going so far as to proclaim consciousness nonexistent.

THE NATURE OF CONSCIOUSNESS

In the Soviet Union, the officially held opinion maintains that consciousness is a *reflection* of objective reality, from which the material attributes of reality itself are absent. In other words, consciousness resembles an image in a mirror. Consciousness is of crucial importance to Soviet psychologists because of their conviction that it is what sets human beings apart from animals. Professor A. H. Leontyev proclaimed that "consciousness cannot be reduced to mere cognitive, thinking processes." He insisted that while animals are capable of thinking and even reasoning, they cannot be termed conscious.

When the Russians use the word *consciousness*, they really mean *self*-consciousness—the ability to observe and evaluate one's own actions, thoughts, and feelings from an outside perspective. This ability requires a certain degree of mental dissociation, whereby one part of the mind acts or feels, while another part observes and evaluates the person who is acting or feeling.

One of the founders of Marxist philosophy, Friedrich Engels, noted that "an animal does not discriminate itself from its activity but is completely immersed in it." Unlike humans, animals do not possess an inner observer to serve as a reflective mirror and provide feedback by which thoughts and actions can be evaluated. Animals do not recognize themselves in a mirror or photograph. When an animal sees its own reflection, it believes it is looking at some other animal.

This perspective maintains that consciousness is not the same as mere thought. It transforms the famous Cartesian notion "I think, therefore I am" into "I am conscious, therefore I am." Indeed, you can be conscious without having any thoughts at all. This fact has made Soviet psychologists draw the line between awareness and consciousness. Sure enough, a dog can be aware of (meaning it has knowledge of) its food or of the presence of its master, but the dog *is not aware of being aware*. The dog cannot be made responsible for what its perceptions relay to its senses.

The way we perceive the content of our consciousness is often determined by our perception of different facets of reality. Thus, different people can see (i.e., be aware of) different facets of the same situation. Example: Three friends are standing on the sidewalk as a man wearing a hat passes by. A gust of wind blows the hat off the man's head, and it is tossed into the middle of the street, where it gets crushed under the wheels of a passing car. One of the observers bursts into laughter. The other is saddened by the plight of the man who has lost his hat. And the third remains neutral; the view just leaves him bored.

Our perceptions of reality—our states of consciousness—are affected by objective reality plus our own predisposition, which influences our observations. This leads to another major principle of Soviet psychology: by altering a person's perception, one can also alter that person's consciousness.

Soviet runner Irina V. became my patient because each competition was plunging her more and more deeply into depression. Her coach believed her to be gifted, but he worried that she might be on the verge of a breakdown. After questioning her, I realized that Irina was so frightened of failure that every time she ran she could think only of what terrible consequences would occur if she didn't win: she would disappoint her country, her coach, her teammates, her parents. "Sometimes I feel I'd be better off dead," she said to me. "That way, no one would be expecting me to win."

Irina's physical strength was being eroded by her bouts of depression. She would tense up and occasionally drop out of races because of painful cramps in her legs and stomach. Irina was almost willing herself to fail.

I decided to attempt to change her perceptions of the race. "Irina," I said, "before every race, I want you to imagine all the people you love waiting for you on the finish line—your mother, your father, your fiancé. Their faces are smiling with anticipation—not because it's a race, but because they cannot wait to hold you in their arms. You need to run this distance to reach them, and if you get there quickly, you will receive their love more quickly too. Imagine that you haven't been home for several months; you will want to race as fast as you can to reach your destination."

Irina replaced her tension-producing perception of the race with an anticipatory, pleasurable perception. Not only did her cramps go away, along with her depression and the idea of herself as a possible failure, but she was able to run faster and better, winning more often and reinforcing her image of herself as a success.

CONTROLLING ATTENTION

In order to alter one's perceptions, it is first necessary to learn how to control and divert one's attention. The nature of attention has always been of great interest to Soviet psychologists. The reason for this is simple: attention is of paramount importance for successful performance, be it for a fighter pilot or a basketball player.

One of the first Russian scientists to probe the origin of attention was Ivan Pavlov. He maintained that in the process of evolution, attention was developed as "the adaptation of an organism to the optimal perception of stimuli." Pavlov indicated that "attention in animals is unintentional, predetermined by the nature of external stimuli." In other words, animals are not free to direct their attention; only humans have the possibility of voluntarily controlling attention.

Attention is the major form in which consciousness exists. No one can be conscious of something without paying attention to it. And, conversely, no one can be attentive to something without being conscious of it. In order to read this book, for example, you must pay attention to its content as well as being conscious of it. If your mind starts drifting into thoughts of tomorrow's appointments, your eyes may continue to slide along the lines but you will no longer be conscious of their content.

It becomes obvious, therefore, that *attention is directed consciousness*. By directing your attention to your TV set (or to your friend's conversation, or to your headache), you are thereby directing your consciousness toward it as well. If you are not in control of your attention, you are not in control of your consciousness, and if you are not in control of your consciousness, you are not in control of your self. Then, for all practical purposes, you are not free; a force other than your self controls your life.

No wonder that in most languages the verb *to listen* can mean "to obey." ("That child just won't listen to anyone.") In Russian, the same adjective, *poslushni*, denotes both "listening" and "obedient."

In Russian psychology, controlling attention has become a key concept. Dr. Victor Alexeev, another of my well-known professors at the Institute, insists that *we can-*

not pay attention to more than one thing at a time. You cannot read and listen to the news simultaneously. You might believe that you have done so, but this illusion is created by the ability of your attention to vacillate rapidly from one topic to another. It's like trying to hit two typewriter keys at the same time; instead of a combination of both letters, you get nothing.

The selective character of attention is based on the suppression of competing stimuli. According to physiologist Dr. A. A. Ukhtomsky,* neurons (nerve cells) operate in either of two modes, inhibition or excitation, a process that can be compared to switching the current off and on in an electrical circuit. These states constantly interact, so that when one area of the cortex in the brain becomes excited, activity in the other areas is inhibited.

Our inability to pay attention to several things at the same time may be partially responsible for the tremendous popularity of TV in America. Often, it's not the actual *attraction* of the shows that keeps us glued to the screen, but the *distraction* of our attention from the dull or painful reality of our own life.

THE POWER OF CONCENTRATION

Certain Russian psychologists, such as Nikolai Trushin and Oleg Sebastyanov, believe that we are not born with the ability to control our attention. Indeed, if you study young children, you will notice that they are unable to concentrate on anything; their attention is scattered and

*See Chapter 7 for a full discussion of the Dominanta Principle.

diffuse. Their actions are erratic, their speech is fragmented, and they often go off on a tangent, forgetting the topic they started to discuss. In fact, children are distinguished by a general lack of consistency.

Attention is fluid, ceaselessly scanning the environment in search of novelty. As Dr. Vladimir Levy has noted, "Motion is the natural condition in which our attention exists." Attention is easily attracted to any new stimulus, be it a sudden noise or an unexpected touch. Any new stimulus exerts a magnetic pull on the attention; this quality in animals ensures their survival by alerting them to possible danger. This is the physiological phenomenon Pavlov has called the "reflex of novelty."

Novelty is the food of attention. After digesting novelty, our attention eagerly searches for new delicacies. Insufficient novelty causes boredom, which compels our attention to switch to something else. If there is nothing else around to feed on, the intensity of attention wanes; one becomes less alert, more drowsy (sleep is the total absence of attention). Thus, boredom offers only two choices: to switch attention to a new stimulus or to fall asleep.

You can recognize an immature person by his tendency to interrupt himself and others, to jump to different topics and be easily distracted. His attention span is very short. As we mature, we learn more and more how to submit our attention to our will. Soviet psychologists claim that one's level of maturity can be measured by the degree to which one can control his or her own attention.

All my life I have been fascinated by the psychology of success. What is it that sets successful men and women apart from the rest? I noticed that all winners have at least one thing in common: an ability to concentrate their attention on a single focus for a long time.

Concentration is all-important to achievement because it adds power to any effort, mental or physical. Many great athletes are notorious for their ability to envelop themselves within a cocoon of concentration. The Olympic jumping champion Viktor Saneev once told me: "When I step on the starting line, everything around me suddenly disappears. I don't hear the fans' voices anymore; I don't see the TV cameras around me; there is nothing on my mind but the finish line."

Successful people report the same double phenomenon described by Saneev: an increased awareness of the object of their concentration, along with a decreased awareness of everything else. I know of boxers who continued fighting with broken ribs without feeling any pain because their attention was wholly absorbed in their performance.

In general, concentration increases the power of any psychological function. When trying to recall a particular point, if you want to add power to your memory, you close your eyes, cutting off disturbing outside stimuli. For the same reason, people close their eyes when kissing, tasting a new food, or having an orgasm.

Concentration of Attention = Concentration of Pleasure

The opposite is true as well: the less conscious you are, the less pleasure you experience. As I sit at my desk finishing this passage, I stretch my hand to pick up the apple I brought from the kitchen a few paragraphs ago. My hand pulls away in disgust as it encounters something small and wet—the core! To my surprise, I realize that the apple got eaten while I was concentrating on my writing. "The apple got eaten," not "I ate the apple," because when your consciousness (attention) is suspended during activity, the activity is automatic, carried out beyond your awareness, not by your conscious self but merely by your animal instincts. Therefore, my use of the passive mode indicates my lack of active participation in the eating process.

One vital step toward becoming a winner lies in learning how to concentrate and focus your attention so as to block out undesirable stimuli. Concentrating your attention also constitutes the foundation for the art of self-control. It is self-control above all that Soviet athletes practice when they win their Olympic medals. In the following section, you will learn how to perform many of the most powerful techniques and exercises we taught our clients at the Moscow Institute.

EXERCISES

Practice these exercises for at least a week, keeping in mind that you must thoroughly master each one before you can allow yourself to progress to the one that follows.

Switching Attention

The object of this exercise is to train you to switch your attention at will and maintain it for a prolonged period of time. This set of exercises, besides being useful by themselves, prepares you for auto-conditioning training, or ACT, which will be covered later in this book (Chapter 6 exercises and Part 2).

- Get two radios. Place one about five feet to your left and another the same distance to your right. Tune to two different stations and adjust the volumes equally to a pleasant, moderate level.
- Sit between the radios with your eyes closed. Visualize your attention as a beam of light emanating from your forehead. Alternate your attention back and forth every twenty seconds from one radio to the other by snapping your fingers. Do this exercise five minutes daily until you reach the goal of being able to concentrate totally on one station while "tuning out" the other.
- Read a book while the news is on the radio. Alternate your attention for about twenty seconds each between reading and listening, and then try to become oblivious to what you are reading while you are listening, and vice versa. Do this for at least five minutes every day until you reach your objective:

total concentration on reading to the total exclusion of the news.

- Learn to become an introvert at will. Imagine turning the beam of your attention inward. While the news is still on the radio, start subtracting in your mind the number 7 from 100. Do this exercise daily until you can become oblivious to the news while subtracting.

Once you have mastered this exercise, start doing similar things with people. For example, if several people are talking to you at the same time, choose which one to listen to and block out the competing voices.

Strengthening Concentration

Sit down by yourself in a room and stare at the second hand of your watch for one minute. See how long you can maintain the following thought: "I am sitting here looking at the hand of the watch." Count how many times your mind veers off from this thought. Repeat this exercise for five minutes every day until you are able to keep your mind completely on this single thought.

Summoning and Manipulating Images

The objective of the following exercises is to develop your ability to summon and manipulate images at will. This in turn helps to develop your concentration and patience.

- Choose some simple object—say, a paper clip. Place this paper clip in the center of a white sheet of paper. Study it meticulously for about three minutes, as if you had never seen anything like it before. Pay attention to its form, texture, and color, trying to absorb in your memory as many details as possible.
- Close your eyes and try to visualize the paper clip for about twenty seconds. The image you get will probably be fuzzy and transitory; usually it will move from the right side to the left. Open your eyes and compare your image with the actual paper clip; notice which of its details your image was missing. Remember that whatever evaded your memory must have evaded your perception as well.
- Now close your eyes again and try to reconstruct the image with the new details you've noticed. Open your eyes and again retrace details your image was missing this time. Close your eyes once more, and repeat the whole procedure. Do this for about five minutes each day until you have reached your goal, which is to keep a sharp and stable image of the paper clip in your mind's eye for at least twenty seconds.
- Develop your objective imagination by learning to manipulate your images. Study an irregular piece of paper from different angles. Then close your eyes and start rotating its image in your mind. How does it look from the side? From the top?
- There are two types of imagination: objective and subjective. An example of *objective imagination* would be to visualize a forest by seeing it from the

outside with your mind's eye. But if you were to imagine yourself walking in this forest, feeling the grass under your feet, smelling the flowers, that would be *subjective imagination*, for you would be a participant in your image.

With this in mind, close your eyes and visualize your paper clip in a stationary position. Then imagine yourself rotating around it, looking at it from various angles. At first, move around it slowly, taking in every detail; then increase the speed, until you begin feeling a bit dizzy.

Producing Body Changes

The following exercise is designed to use the power of your imagination to produce actual physiological changes in your body.

Place your right index finger on a sheet of paper. Repeat the procedure you followed when you first contemplated the paper clip (study the details of your finger, then close your eyes and try to see it, and so on). The only difference in this finger exercise is in regard to the location of your image. Whereas the image of the paper clip would be somewhere around your head (usually it is a few inches in front of your forehead), the image of your index finger should coincide with the finger itself. When you close your eyes and try to "see" your finger, its image should be inside the finger itself, where it lies on the piece of paper. In the previous exercises you took your paper clip into your consciousness, while with the finger exercise you place the image of your finger into the finger itself (i.e., you bring your consciousness to your finger).

The success of this exercise will manifest itself in various physical sensations in your finger: you may start experiencing pulsation, warmth, needles-and-pins, or itching.

Although they may seem simple, remember that these are the same attention-control techniques Soviet sports psychologists have used to propel award-winning athletes through one Olympic victory after another. Not only are superior powers of concentration vital to success in any endeavor, but competitors who can control their perceptions of reality can turn any situation to their advantage.

5 THE KEY TO SELF-CONTROL

In order to transcend all previous performance limits, Soviet psychologists feel it is essential for individuals to gain mastery of their physical, mental, and emotional selves.

SELF-CONTROL: THE SECRET OF SUCCESS

At the Moscow Institute, we ran a personality test on hundreds of successful individuals from various walks of life. To our amazement, we discovered that almost eighty percent of them possessed no more than average mental abilities and were devoid of outstanding creativity. But they all shared one quality: self-control.

It has also become apparent that the greatest "failures" were people endowed with unusual gifts. Highly intelligent students, used to reaping all the prizes without having to make a sustained effort, failed to develop their self-control. Later in life, they watched helplessly as less gifted but more diligent individuals overtook them on the road to success.

Lev Alburt, one of the leading Soviet chess grand masters, told me, "Most human problems seem to be tied to self-control. Everything points to this common factor. Whether you're jealous, afraid, timid, or drink too much, the common link seems to be an absence of self-control."

Samorazvitie psychology—the Soviet answer to the West's human potential movement—also pinpoints lack of self-control as the most widespread problem influencing the physical, emotional, and mental lives of normal people. Russian psychologists note that a lack of efficiency in controlling one's *bodily* functions can cause such problems as tremors, stuttering, muscle spasms, and hypertension. Failure to master one's *emotional* functions results in such common disorders as anxiety, fear, irritability, envy, shyness, and laziness. Weakening of control in the *mental* realm leads to the appearance of obsessive ideas, muddy thinking, blocked creativity, scatteredness, impatience, and procrastination. In addition, Soviet psychologists are convinced that when problems overlap from one category into another, addictive patterns may develop, such as drug abuse, alcoholism, overeating, and compulsive sexuality.

Dr. Vladimir Levy, a leading authority on the *samorazvitie* movement, maintains that "no one can govern himself in every situation, and, conversely . . . no human being is always out of control." Indeed, we all possess some areas where our self-control is stronger and some where it is weaker. Ivan, a boxer, could practice for hours at a time in the gym but blew up at what he considered criticism every time his coach tried to make suggestions on how to improve his fight. Maria, a swimmer, seemed unable to perform unless her legs were smoothly shaved and her hands neatly manicured;

the slightest imperfection in her appearance caused her to hyperventilate. I have known brilliant doctors who were unable to stop smoking, and otherwise disciplined individuals who could not stick to a weight-loss diet.

THE BRUTON AND THE SUPRON

Considering that each of us has an Achilles' heel in the realm of self-control, how can we strengthen the areas in which we are weakest? Soviet psychology is based on the premise that almost any human problem can be solved by strengthening one's self-control. Of course, the very word *control* implies the presence of a subject (the controller) and an object (the controllee). If I say, "Boris controls his horse," it's obvious that I mean Boris is the controller and the horse is being controlled. But what do I mean when I say, "You have good self-control"? Which part of you is the rider, and which is the horse?

The noted Russian psychologist Lev Vigotsky first made the principal distinction betwen "lower," or natural, mental functions and "higher," cultural, functions, which are specifically human and appear gradually in the course of our development. In a mature psyche, the lower functions are structured and organized by the higher functions, according to specifically human social goals.

For the sake of clarity, lets label the lower mental functions *Bruton*, and the higher mental functions *Supron*. In the context of Russian psychology, Bruton encompasses our instincts and natural drives—everything we were born with. Supron, in turn, represents uniquely human attributes like language, moral standards, and consciousness. Thus, here is an answer to our previous question: it is our Supron that does the controlling and our Bruton that is the controllee.

Although you are composed of both Bruton and Supron, what you refer to as your "self" is in fact your Supron—your higher values, your consciousness. The Bruton can be compared to a coiled spring that must constantly be pushed down by your Supron if you want to be an achiever. Your Bruton lies coiled up like a greedy animal, ready to spring out and seize the moment. The more space you allow it to take, the less remains available to your Supron. And the balance between these two represents the degree of your self-control.*

In the personal struggle for self-control, Soviet psychology warns us, it is imperative to become aware of these polar forces battling within us. Learning to discern the origin of our desires and actions is the first step toward exerting mastery over them. It is when we forget that we are actually of two minds that we begin to ascribe all our motives to the Supron, to our willful self, and the result is confusion and frustration.

Take my patient Tamara, a former Olympic swimmer. "When I got married," she confessed, biting her fingernails with ill-concealed anxiety, "I quit sports altogether. Within months, I had gained forty pounds. When the scale hit one-sixty, I decided to give up all fattening foods. Except—and this was the worst of it for me—chocolate. I had never been able to resist it, and suddenly I found

*There is a principal difference between the Freudian notion of Id-Ego and the notion of Bruton-Supron. Freud labeled as Id everything contained in the subconscious mind, while Bruton contains only those drives and instincts we possess before birth. Everything we acquire after birth is labeled Supron.

myself gobbling down two, three bars a day, hiding the wrappers so my husband wouldn't catch me."

With genuine incredulity, she turned to me and exclaimed, "Why am I behaving this way? I know I want to lose weight, but every day I find myself crying out for chocolate, and I'm not satisfied until I've consumed at least one entire bar! I don't understand."

I explained to Tamara that the two forces within her were fighting for control over her actions. While her Supron wanted her to diet, her Bruton, like a willful child, was seeking to break that resolve and indulge its own craving for sweets. How were we to put Supron in control?

I formulated a theory for Tamara. Her body could not be termed her "self." It was her Supron—her center of willful activity—that, regulating her body, made her a person. To strengthen Tamara's Supron, I told her, we first needed to separate it from Bruton, which otherwise would continue to pull it down and vanquish Supron's determination to do what was right for Tamara as a human being.

"Your Bruton belongs to you, like your clothes and your books; but it is not you," I pointed out. "If you received a kidney transplant, you would still be yourself, wouldn't you? But if your brain died and your body were kept alive through machines, that body would not really be you, would it? It would simply be a thing, like your dress or your favorite watch."

Unlike the predominant Western theories that glorify the so-called "wisdom of the body" and encourage us to follow its impulses, the Russians believe that our body is quite dumb. Professor L. E. Ruvinsky of Moscow has elaborated on this idea. The instincts controlling the body's reactions are built-in, automatic programs sustained by the "hard wiring" between neurons in the old brain center (paleocortex). As a result, Ruvinsky maintains, our instinctual knowledge is often inappropriate and counterproductive.

Explaining all this to Tamara brought her behavior into focus. Tamara's body—stupidly, constantly—urged her on to self-destruction. Overcoming the temptation to give in to its pressures would prove difficult but not impossible. First she had to learn how to strengthen the mechanism (willpower) with which her higher self could bear down on her Bruton's blind instincts.

I set up a program for Tamara consisting of a weekly weight-loss goal coupled with a diet and a series of rigorous exercises she was to perform each day. Also, I devised a mental game that would reinforce Tamara's self-control. I told her that every time her Supron won against her Bruton, she was to reward herself with a little treat. Since Tamara loved pretty nightgowns, I instructed her to set aside money each week and purchase a new gown each time her Supron won and she reached her weekly weight-loss goal. Each time her Bruton won and she failed to reach her goal, she was to spend the money on something she hated, like household cleaning materials.

By this simple positive reinforcement, Tamara's willpower increased as her self-control was strengthened. Soon she began to take pride in her ability not to give in to her Bruton. She realized that her true self was her Supron, and she felt good about its ability to conquer her cravings. The little game she had learned to play with herself may have been childish, but it worked. Sometimes, in order to tame the childish Bruton, we must use childish means.

In the Soviet Union, taming one's Bruton is often accomplished by enduring pain. The ideal of the Spartans, who lived an ascetic existence in ancient Greece, is emulated in the molding of young Russians. As a schoolboy in Rostov, I often watched a uniquely Soviet game of self-control. Old men on the street would offer to the public a so-called *silomer* (strength measurer). The device consisted of a battery and a pair of heavy copper electrodes connected to a potentiometer, which allowed the flow of electricity through a conductive object. If two individuals decided to challenge each other, they would pay ten kopecks to an old man, who would hook up one of the challengers and gradually turn up the electric current until the pain could no longer be endured. Then he would do the same thing to the second man, and the results would be compared. The man who had endured the most pain was pronounced the winner, garnering the respect and cheers of the crowd that always gathered to watch the contest.

In daily life, too, it is often Bruton's blind, instinctive avoidance of pain and effort that Supron must master in order to exert self-control. This is exactly the situation I faced during my first encounter with aerobics. My friend Vickie, who taught five classes a day, finally prevailed upon me to attend one of her workout sessions. After fifteen minutes of bizarre and strenuous movement, my aching body decided to surrender. It slid down to the floor, breathing heavily, telling me in no uncertain terms, "Get the hell out of here!" The command was strong and compelling, and for a moment I felt myself weakening and yielding, almost humiliated. And then those feelings sparked a rebellion. "Come on, you quitter!" I shouted at my body. "Get up and endure, in spite of the pain!" Forcing myself up, I continued with the session.

At the end of the class, my legs wobbly and my head still spinning, I made my way to Vickie, who looked for all the world as if she'd just awakened from a refreshing nap. "Well?" she demanded. "How do you feel?"

"Exhilarated and proud of myself," I confided. And I walked out into the sunshine, determined, for the first time, to quit smoking. My rather unexpected ability to endure an entire aerobics class had given me the confidence that the Supron in me could be stronger than my rebellious, catankerous, ever-prankish Bruton, that up until then had won many battles.

The Ripple Effect

Dr. Leonid Gissen of the Moscow Institute told us that self-control, like all the "higher talents," is an acquired skill, whose development can be compared to that of a muscle. "If you exercise it diligently, you will develop its strength," he told us, "but if you let it slide, it will soon stop functioning."

According to Gissen, there is a ripple effect involved in developing self-control. A person who learns to exert self-control in one area of life will automatically feel equipped to take on another. When I had persisted through Vickie's aerobics class, I had felt strong enough to give up cigarettes, a habit that had controlled me since my arrival in the United States.

Vickie herself embodies the ripple effect of self-control. Overweight since childhood, Vickie decided in her twenties to lose eighty pounds. After a careful diet that lasted nearly a year, the weight came off and stayed off permanently. Having conquered her addiction to junk food and overeating, Vickie was then able to tackle a rigorous schedule of aerobic exercises to tighten her sagging muscles.

The High Is Psychological

If the Russian view of these matters is correct, it is the striving for better self-control that lies at the heart of the efforts of millions of runners, bodybuilders, and other athletes. They are primarily *mindbuilders*, finding internal reward in extending the boundaries of their endurance and power. The reward, I believe, is the cause of the so-called runner's high, not endorphins. I agree with Dr. Robert McMurray of the University of North Carolina, who wrote in the *Journal of Applied Physiology*, "If there is such a thing as runner's high, it is not being caused by endorphins. . . . The attraction of prolonged exercise is probably psychological."

Most people are not aware that physical well-being may not be the only benefit they gain from spending so many hours sweating in the gym or running on the trail. Many fail to notice a mental gain from physical exercise. Thus Dr. Christiaan Barnard, the pioneer of human heart transplants, once mentioned that "if joggers did not have the opportunity to run, they would rather be whipped instead!" William Zinsser of the *New York Times* even described joggers as "self-confident prisoners of fitness." He could see, he said, no joy on their faces, only duty and pain.

THROUGH WILL TO SELF-MASTERY

Will is the cornerstone of self-control; it regulates all voluntary activities of a human being. According to Soviet psychologists, will is the human capacity to execute one's conscious decisions. The will is viewed as the executive representative of one's self, one's Supron.

Animals don't possess will, for there can be no will without consciousness. Any willful action must be preceded by the image of the goal and the means to attain it, which entails being conscious of what one is doing and of the action's consequences. By ignoring consciousness, Western behaviorists also ignore the vast realm of free will and its ramifications.

Only consciousness allows human beings to see ahead to their goal, to plan the steps that will implement this feat. Only self-control can prevent one's Bruton from destroying one's resolution (as with Tamara, until she was trained to exercise and develop the power of her will). Therefore, we can formulate the Soviet view in a simple equation:

Self-Control = Consciousness + Will

Animals have no will with which to delay or suppress their innate drives and reactions (their Brutons). The same is true of infants; we are not born with self-control, but acquire it along with other learned human skills. Both animals and human infants are subject to their drives and are therefore not free to choose other responses. Mature human beings, however, have a choice.

Willful suppression of one's innate drives, one's Bruton, is the key to success and survival. It also determines the level of an individual's maturity. Lev Alburt, the chess grand master, can remain intent on his game for as long as seven hours. During that time, neither his body's innate drives to eat, sleep, or urinate nor the acknowledgment of extraneous noises and occurrences distract his concentration. Because his self-control has been exercised so often over the past twenty years, Alburt has reduced his Bruton to a manageable size. Compared with Tamara, whose rapacious Bruton was too strong to ignore, Alburt is a highly developed, mature individual, able to direct his attention at will however he chooses.

Of course, even the most highly developed individual's self-control has a tendency to fluctuate. At times you may feel that you are absolutely helpless to govern yourself, while there are moments when you feel 100 percent in control.

Two factors cause self-control to oscillate. The first is our level of emotional arousal. On one extreme is the state of rapture, the peak of excitement; on the other is sleep, in which a person is almost totally without consciousness. It is the area in the middle, when a person is relaxed but aware, where self-control is strongest. As Vladimir Levy tells us, "A person in deep sleep is as helpless as the one in convulsions, possessed by panic, or passionate love." The second factor that throws our self-control out of kilter is frustration of bodily needs. Every time our body is distressed, it exerts more pressure on our Supron, our self-control. Obviously, our self-control diminishes when we are hungry, thirsty, sleepy, tired, sick, sexually deprived, and so on.

Let's say you and your teenage daughter are driving to the airport to pick up a friend. On the freeway, the traffic begins to slow and you are caught in a bottleneck, crawling along at five miles per hour. As the minutes tick by, you grow more and more distressed, imagining your friend waiting impatiently on the sidewalk outside the baggage area. What is he thinking? Might he conclude that you won't arrive, and take a taxi in the meantime?

The air in the car has gone stale, and you crack open the window. Outside, the freeway exudes traffic noises and fumes, which set off a migraine in your head. Your dashboard clock tells you it is past dinnertime, and you begin to feel hunger pangs. To make things even worse, you're dying to use a toilet. Horns explode in a cacophony of sounds that pierce your head like sharp drills, worsening your headache. You are feeling absolutely miserable . . . and not very human.

Innocently, your daughter turns to you and asks if you have a piece of gum. That's the last straw! All at once, the sum total of your frustrations give way, and you scream. Your Bruton has just triumphed, overpowering your Supron's balanced sense of fairness.

The reverse is also true. Say you've decided to give up smoking. Your resoluteness carries you through many temptations, and you gain confidence in your willpower. After one month of abstinence, a friend happens to offer you a puff on his cigarette. Confident that you have overcome your addiction and craving, you tell yourself, "Why not? After all, I won't be smoking out of need, only out of pleasure. And it's just one puff!"

Following your inner voice, you inhale deeply. At the moment your will wavers, your Bruton, coiled and ready, springs forward and topples your Supron. The dam of your resistance (your will) breaks and the mass of your Bruton urge rushes through like a tidal wave, destroying all vestiges of self-control. Overpowered by your Bruton, you find yourself smoking the whole cigarette, then another, and finally the entire pack. We can call this phenomenon the "first straw."

Some people push self-control beyond the sensible. To be a well-balanced human being, one cannot cage Bruton all the time. We are, after all, comprised of both our instincts and our learned behavior. If you scare your Bruton into paralysis, its spring will rust and your instincts will partially atrophy. We have all run across such supercerebral individuals and been struck by their frigid personalities.

Proponents of iron-fisted determination should keep in mind that one of the most important qualities of self-control is the ability to let it go, to abandon oneself to pleasure, feelings, unguarded thoughts. If we don't let go at times, our creativity will be hampered, and we may miss out on these valuable peaks in experience that inspire us to push ourselves beyond mediocrity.

Some people with excessive self-control have tamed their Bruton out of fear. They have felt it spring out, overpowering all their faculties, and now they keep it in check the way a parent would control a rebellious, destructive teenager by grounding him. The price is spontaneity.

Such people who cannot allow their Brutons any freedom fall prey to excessive premeditation and calculation. Overly self-controlled, they tend to be mentally rigid, unable to change or adapt to altered conditions or new strategies. They view this changing world through overcautious eyes, imagining each uncertainty as a threat of danger. Such people become overregimented, leaving themselves no room for anything that has not been programmed down to the last cent of their budget or minute of their schedule. The phrase that frightens them the most is likely to be "Let's play it by ear," for they have no conception of free-flowing emotion or light improvisation. Against a more adaptable or imaginative opponent, they are inevitably doomed to failure and defeat.

THE NECESSITY OF ACTION

Soviet psychologists believe that the most frequent problem holding people back from their full potential is the gap between their intentions and their actions. The Soviets believe that it's better not to possess talent at all than to possess it without utilizing it. The primordial importance of action in Soviet thought can be traced to Dr. Ivan Sechenov, who wrote:

> The infinite diversity of external manifestations of cerebral activity can be reduced ultimately to a single phenomenon—muscular movement. Whether it is a child's laughing at the sight of a toy, or Garibaldi's smiling when prosecuted for excessive love of his native land, or a girl's trembling at the first thought of love, or Newton's creating universal laws and inscribing them on paper—the ultimate fact in all cases is muscular movement.

Thoughts and feelings, therefore, are given life only through muscular movement of some kind, through action. Writing and speaking are actions. A word is an action. In a court of law, words are held as actions, and people can be scarred through words as deeply as through physical violence. A word can kill . . . and a word can heal. An action gives objective, three-dimensional existence, as well as temporal duration, to a thought. The life span of a thought is measured in seconds, while a deed or a written word can last millennia.

The "execution of correct actions," Konstantin Stanislavsky wrote, "will bring about the correct feelings or emotions in the actor." He believed that actions were in some ways superior to, and could be used to control, feelings and thought. B. F. Skinner, the Western behaviorist, held much the same view when he encouraged a depressed person to change his or her facial expression into a smile. Skinner found that this muscular movement alone often triggered a corresponding lift in mood. This same technique has long been employed by Soviet psychiatrists, many of whom have never even heard of behaviorists!

Soviet psychologists believe that the gap between decision and action can result from a difference in energies. They maintain that there are two basic kinds of energy, physical and mental. The well-rounded person possesses them in more or less equal amounts. Others may be prolific on a mental level, bubbling with great ideas and projects, but have not developed their physical energies sufficiently, resulting in apathy or inertia that prevents them from converting plans into reality. They need to develop their physical self-control just as others need to develop their mental self-control.

Part 2 of this book will present exercises designed to strengthen both mental and physical self-control.

STRENGTH AND DURATION OF WILL

Russian psychiatrists T. Zayzev and N. Prokhorov distinguish two main components in successful self-control: strength and duration. The *strength* of one's will is measured by the amount of effort one is capable of exerting to overcome an obstacle. A weightlifter is usually endowed with this type of explosive strength. The *duration*, however, is measured by time; i.e., how long one is capable of sustaining the effort. A marathon runner must possess this kind of sustained self-control.

Let me reemphasize the critical role self-control plays in self-esteem. When you control your Bruton, your Supron (your self) feels proud and strong. You can tell a lot about the degree of self-control by observing how people hold themselves and how they look. The side of themselves they display to the outer world is not likely to deviate from their self-image. A slender woman with well-groomed hands, clean attractive hair, and tasteful clothes displays the control necessary to keep up her appearance. Similarly, an overweight man with a stubbly beard, dirty hair, and unkempt clothes displays not only lack of self-control but also lack of self-esteem.

If your self-esteem is strong and resilient, you will not allow an incidental failure to pull you down. You may lose some battles along the way, but your ability to push on, without letting your self-control slip away in despair, will hold you to your winning course. In Russia, we call this the Golden Triad: learn from your mistake, don't dwell on it, and then start anew with even greater strength.

EXERCISES

The following exercises are designed to increase your general capacity for self-control. Only by suppressing the urges of the Bruton can your Supron accomplish its chosen goals. For it is the ability to concentrate on one's goals and to carry them out that distinguishes winners from losers.

But, you may wonder, how can you be sure you have the self-control to follow through on these exercises? What if you are so low in self-control that you can't even do these exercises consistently?

The following two exercises are designed with just such a person in mind. They require almost no effort. The simplicity of the activities is designed to discourage the temptation to skip a single one, because skipping "just this once" is guaranteed to create a momentum of failure. Even a tiny crack in the pillar of your self-resolution can cause the whole construction to collapse.

Useless-Routine Exercise

Most of our actions pursue a certain practical purpose, from stretching a hand toward a glass of water to hammering a nail. But how about doing something without *any* practical purpose, simply to exercise and increase your willpower?

Set yourself some arbitrary, purposeless task once a day. It can be anything from putting a photograph face down in the morning and up at night, to placing a sock over your lamp at 8:00 P.M. The sillier or more useless it is, the better. A patient of mine used to place a left shoe in a cupboard every morning and touch her right ear at noon.

The major factor in the success of this exercise is choosing an action that can be done easily. Any strain must be avoided, because the goal is not to strengthen will but to sustain an action repeatedly during a prolonged period of time. In other words, do something extremely easy, but do it *regularly*.

We all perform certain actions regularly, out of habit: brush our teeth, get dressed, and so on. All these rituals have by now become unconscious. But consciously choosing your own rituals will serve to strengthen the pillars of your self-reliance.

Echo-Magnet

This exercise, developed by Dr. Vladimir Levy, the Soviet authority on self-control, is designed to ease the strain that results from the intense effort of working at something you consider important. The Echo-Magnet is a quick, effective method for easily commencing and sustaining any activity.

In general, there are two kinds of necessities: external and internal. External necessity consists of all the things forced on us by life; it is expressed in the form of a "I must": "I must do my homework," "I must be polite," "I must do the wash," and on and on. No wonder the satisfaction of external necessity is often connected with strain and displeasure. Conversely, internal necessity consists of all the things that make life livable, expressed in the form of "I want": "I want a new car," "I want to get some rest,"

"I want to be happy." The tasks to satisfy these wants are approached with zest and pleasure.

By using the Echo-Magnet exercise, you can convert your "musts" into "wants."

The Echo-Magnet has three stages:

1. An emphatic command to yourself (stated with a lot of passion, pressure, drive).
2. Becoming truly empty and relaxed, ridding yourself of the slightest thought, until you achieve a state of total serenity.
3. Eliciting your ascending will.

Let's say you are sitting at the table, trying to start writing a report, staring at a pile of white paper. You feel a certain legitimate aversion to the task, which seems to be beyond your capabilities as well as interest.

Now it's time to start the Echo-Magnet exercise. Close your eyes and say, "I must write, I **must write**" (repeat eight times). Whisper it with ever-escalating fervor, until you reach a passionate crescendo, a demand. Then stop abruptly and let yourself flop back in your chair in a state of complete relaxation.

Now try to summon total indifference to the project, as you whisper, "**I don't want to write**" (repeat five times). Again build to passionate demand. Try to feel an emptiness, devoid of any trace of striving.

After about a minute, notice that something starts reverberating deep within you, and you will find yourself feeling: "**I want to write!**" (repeat it eight times).

Notice how saying the phrase gradually begets a feeling—a feeling of potency, of energy that restlessly wants to express itself in action. Once you start feeling this urge, grab your pen and start writing your report, riding along on the wave of this desire to write.

Keep in mind a wise triad formulated by Stanislavsky: "Make the difficult habitual: what is habitual will become easy, and what is easy will become agreeable."

As you progress in your exercise, become aware of the general increase in your self-control, which will manifest itself in various areas of your life. Remeber that even a small victory over yourself makes you much stronger.

Let the words of William James serve as an inspiration in your new endeavor: "Be systematically heroic every day in little unnecessary things."

6 ACHIEVING A STATE OF OPTIMAL FUNCTIONING

Soviet research seems to have proved that states of inspired functioning are not the province of the few, but can be tapped and achieved by everybody.

Dr. Leonid Gissen, my professor at the Moscow Research Institute of Physical Culture, and his colleagues were convinced that each human being possesses the power to bring about peak performance at will. At the Institute we labeled this magic state SOF, for *state of optimal functioning*, because the term *inspiration* was too vague and had become muddied by millennia of myths and misconceptions. Being firmly convinced that this state arises from within the individual and not without, we conducted a series of experiments in our lab. We asked athletes to recall their greatest SOF and then to verbalize all accompanying sensations in great detail.

After sifting the data through a computer, we found that all the subjects reported a special feeling of facility and effortlessness, when everything seemed to happen with unusual ease and precision, "just by itself." A basketball player felt that the basket itself "just pulled the ball right into it." A runner experienced a wonderful state of lightness and vigor as if he were being propelled to the finish line by a strong gust of wind blowing at his back. My client Viktor Saneev, after establishing his world record in the triple jump, told me in awe: "I couldn't believe the results; I wasn't even trying hard—it seemed so damn easy for me!"

One explanation for this sensation lies in the fact that at such times, our subjects reported they were completely absorbed by their activity. They were acting wholeheartedly, without self-doubt or hesitation. They were totally possessed by a feeling of rightness and sureness, which endowed their action with unusual precision.

Our research at the Institute showed that the SOF is elicited by the interactions of three main characteristics: physical, emotional, and mental.

PHYSICAL CHARACTERISTICS OF SOF

The physical sensations accompanying SOF vary greatly from person to person. The Russian world-champion weightlifter, Vassili Alexeev, once confided to me that, when inspired, he usually experiences tingling sensations in his jaw as well as dryness in his mouth. Other athletes report such diverse physical symptoms as coolness at the temples, a feeling of emptiness in the pit of the stomach, tears in the eyes, a lump in the throat. Rifle marksmen are known to have dilated pupils during competition, a condition that ensures sharper vision.

In the USSR, we were directed to pick out key reactions in our athletes. Wrestlers, for example, are very sensitive to how they feel in relation to the ground. They try to capture the sensation of being balanced, or grounded, by becoming aware of their center of gravity. If they feel slightly unsteady, they begin to shuffle their feet. Likewise, you can tell that a basketball player is anxious before shooting a key free throw if he shuffles his feet at the free-throw line.

Experienced athletes are familiar with their own physical cues, although they are rarely able to evoke them voluntarily. It is up to the sports psychologist to teach them this discipline, which often merely brings to light what the athletes already fundamentally know but either ignore or overlook.

A boxer will often try to reach his optimal rhythm, the vibrating sensation in his whole body. When I was working with a young boxer, I asked him before each fight to tap his hand on the desk at his most comfortable rhythm; it usually turned out to be about 20 percent faster that his pulse rate. Similarly, boxers who know their optimal rhythms often listen to music with an appropriate beat right before a match.

Another physical phenomenon people often experience in SOF is fusion with their equipment. The foil seems to become a continuation of the fencer's arm; the same goes for baseball players with their bats, marksmen with their rifles, surgeons with their scalpels, musicians with their instruments. They all report transcending the boundaries of their bodies, becoming a single unit with their equipment.

Martial artists and wrestlers often experience merging with their opponents in a kind of physical empathy.

As the Russian wrestler Anatoly Topolev described it to me: "When I am at my best, I feel a kind of oneness with my rival. I become able to predict his every motion, and I feel I can move his body with almost the same ease with which I move my own."

I was always in awe while observing the great Russian cellist Mstislav Rostropovich when he was in his SOF. He seemed to be embracing his cello, gently squeezing it, tenderly goading it on . . . almost as though he were making love to it. He did not look like a musician playing an instrument—instead, the two had combined into a complex music-producing unit.

Other SOF sensations described by athletes included feeling "light as a bird." Most of those we interviewed described feeling their forehead expanding, and their head tended to be poised upward and to the right.

EMOTIONAL CHARACTERISTICS OF SOF

People experience a wide range of positive emotions when in SOF, from mild elation through exhilaration, playfulness, joy, serenity, and bliss. However, some find it useful to evoke such negative emotions as anger and rage.

Many boxers perform better if they can generate hatred for their opponents, to fuel aggressive endurance during the fight. Remember the insults Muhammad Ali shouted at his rivals prior to his matches? Some tennis players seem to conjure up similar feelings during competition, such as "bad boys" Jimmy Connors and John McEnroe. Fear can sometimes serve as a motivational factor. Seventeen-year-old British swimmer Steve Holland discovered his optimal emotion while observing the fish in his aquarium. "Once," he said, "I tapped on the wall of the aquarium and watched the fish fearfully dashing away at high speed. I thought to myself, What if, while swimming, I imagined being chased by a shark?" He tried it and established two world records.

Then there's the case of a Russian ski-plane pilot, grounded in Siberia while repairing his skis. When he felt something brush his shoulder, he waved away what he thought was his copilot, suspecting a prank. When the push was repeated, he whirled around—and confronted a polar bear. In an instant, the pilot was atop the wing of his plane, yelling for help (which arrived promptly). Later he tried to repeat this jump and found that he could barely make it halfway. Measuring the distance from the ground to the wing, he discovered that it was close to the world high-jump record.

In general, it seems that any strong emotion possesses energy that can be employed to boost performance. This might be the reason behind some unusual feats of strength and stamina that arise from emergency situations. We all have heard of cases in which women of average strength were able, after an accident, to lift cars to rescue their children, and of mediocre swimmers who have swum for miles to reach shore after a shipwreck.

Even grief over personal tragedy can trigger SOF. My client Vera H. played an important violin concert at the Odessa Philharmonic just after she had learned of her mother's death. "I don't remember how I got to the stage," she told me later. "The tears couldn't stop flowing, like veils blocking my vision. But when I started to play, I felt a sudden, tremendous release, expressing my pain through the music." Critics unequivocally agreed that she gave the best performance of her career that night.

The Biochemical Response

What enables these hidden powers to emerge? At the Institute we tested top athletes by taking samples of their blood and urine before and after a workout at the stadium and by putting electrodes on them during and after an exceptional performance. We discovered that every strong emotion causes complex biochemical reactions in the body: increased secretion of adrenaline and blood sugar, inhibition of the digestive system (to make more blood available for the working muscles). But the most important is the lowering of the threshold of motor responses—the increased excitability of the muscles by nervous impulses, which results in powerful movement.

Any strong stimulus has a potential to rocket the individual toward the heights of performance. Overstimulation of any sense organ can carry with it the possibility of SOF. It can come from anything: intense and prolonged sound (music, a scream, a siren); intense body movement (runner's high, prolonged dancing); intense light (strobe lights in a disco). Anything that shakes your mind strongly enough possesses the power to break down the boundaries of your habitual thought patterns, your habitual behavior, to release an energy you never dreamed of having.

When for some reason muscular activity becomes impossible during an emergency, the energy released by the emotions turns inward against one's body. "Emotion without motion" can often cause a heart attack or a stroke, which is why it is crucial to work off or at least "shake off" the surplus energy caused by stress.

Physiologically, the effect that various emotions can have on performance comes down to the level of emotional arousal or, more simply, the level of anxiety. Many Western athletes and coaches believe that anxiety is detrimental to performance, but this is not so: if you have no anxiety, you become lethargic and apathetic. Some American sports psychologists seem to miss this point, directing all their efforts toward relaxing an athlete before the competition. Their Russian counterparts, on the other hand, try to induce an optimal level of anxiety in each athlete.

Pulse and Anxiety

It is simple to determine when you have reached your own optimal level of anxiety: just count your pulse. Your pulse rate is in direct relation to your anxiety, your level of excitement.

According to Dr. Alexeev of the Institute, the best way to discover your optimal level of anxiety is to take your pulse three minutes before a crucial activity (write the rate down in a diary) and compare it with your subsequent performance.

If you are a runner, take your pulse before a race. Let's say it's 90 beats per minute. Then write down your result—imagine that it was one minute, thirty seconds, per mile. Next time you take your pulse, it might be 110, with a one-minute, twenty-second mile. The third time your pulse might be 130, with a one-minute, forty-second mile. Now let's look at how these figures can point to SOF:

PULSE	PERFORMANCE
90	1′30″
110	1′20″
130	1′40″

Since your best performance (1′20″) corresponds with a pulse rate of 110, this is your optimal pulse rate.

Next time you are about to compete (or go on a job interview, a special date, or whatever), take your pulse. If it is slower than your optimal rate, speed it up; if it is faster, slow it down. There are several ways of doing this. The most efficient one is through auto-conditioning training (ACT), which will be outlined in the Exercise section of this chapter. ACT includes a discipline of mental commands that will eventually make your body and heart respond almost automatically, producing you optimal pulse rate at will.

A simpler way of producing your optimal pulse rate is learning how to pace your physical movement. This technique is less effective than ACT in that it provides immediate gratification without forming a habitual pattern through training, but it can help in an emergency when you don't have time for an entire ACT routine. If you need to slow down your pulse and reduce your anxiety level, try slow stretching combined with slow rhythmic breathing and prolonged exhalations. To speed up your pulse rate, jump rope at a fast pace while keeping your breathing rapid and shallow.

Soviet sports psychologists sometimes employ techniques that go against the moral grain of Westerners. The truth is that in the USSR, morals tend to be bent to suit the occasion. While I do not condone this practice in the area of politics or human rights, I have found that in sports, making the athlete just angry enough to win a competition can be quite effective.

I remember a skeet-shooting tournament in my native town of Rostov, in which I was advising the world-renowned markswoman Natasha Penkova. That day her performance was not up to her usual masterful level; something was off. During a break I took her aside and measured her pulse. It was 84. Knowing that her optimal rate was about 130, I decided to use a little trick.

"Give me your rifle," I said brusquely. She surrendered her weapon to me with surprise on her face.

"And now," I continued in the same tone of voice, "run quickly to that tree and back." I pointed to a birch tree a few hundred meters away.

"Why?" she asked hesitantly.

"Don't ask me why," I muttered in an irritated tone, "just do it!"

Natasha bit her lip, then turned around and ran. After she returned, I noticed that she was angry with me; her cheeks were flushed and her eyes were sparkling with indignation. I took her pulse again: 135.

"Now you are okay," I smiled encouragingly at her. "Grab your rifle and go; it is your turn to shoot."

Her face began to brighten with understanding. She winked at me and dashed to the shooting line. It wasn't long before the referees announced her the winner.

Natasha understood that while I had in a sense manipulated her, my intent had been anything but malicious. Of course, there are limits. A sports psychologist who shouts racial slurs at his client in order to make the athlete's pulse rate jump goes too far. This is both unethical and cruel. But a good sports psychologist or a good manager must understand his or her client well enough to know how to push just a little bit to motivate victory, without causing the client any harm. At the Institute, we used this method whenever necessary to help bring about the desire level of anxiety in our more apathetic athletes.

MENTAL CHARACTERISTICS OF SOF

Many of the athletes I have worked with throughout the years were in superb physical shape and filled with the best competitive spirit. Yet they failed to achieve good results. Why? They did not have the right thoughts.

Every performance has two components: the goal and the means. For example, the goal of a marksman is to hit the bull's-eye. The means are to choose the right body position, to line up the sights and the target, to ensure extreme stability of the hand, to hold one's breath while pulling the trigger smoothly. But should the marksman direct attention toward the goal or the means?

The Soviet athletes I worked with, as well as the American competitors whom I helped prepare for the Los Angeles Olympics, often asked me an apparently simple question: "What are we supposed to think while performing?" Let's try to answer this question, keeping in mind that in sports, "to think of" usually means "to pay attention to." So the question might well be: "What should an athlete pay attention to while competing?"

It is almost always best to concentrate on the means. When you faithfully follow every necessary step, you inevitably reach your goal. As Gandhi put it, "Take care of the means, and the end will take care of itself."

Don't forget: you cannot pay attention to two different things simultaneously. Any attention you fix on the goal detracts from the attention you have available for the means. Forget this golden rule of psychology and you are throwing away an important edge in performance.

My client Turischeva learned this the hard way. She had to turn in a perfect performance on the horizontal bars to ensure victory for the entire Russian gymnastics team. But while preparing for the vault, all she could think about was the bar. "It was a mistake," she told me later. "I failed the vault."

Experienced marathon runners continuously monitor all aspects of their race. By focusing on the means, they can win the race one element at a time, each element directed toward the goal: Am I going too fast or too slowly? How much energy do I have left? Is this a serious pain in my ankle, or just a passing ache? Where are my main competitors?

Modern society trains people to be goal-oriented and to view the process of getting there as an inevitable evil, a chore that must be plowed through to reach the desired end. But once you win the game, the game is over. Of course, there is no game without a goal, but the real goal is success in the process. While fear of getting there represents a definite neurosis, so does the notion that the goal is everything and the process negligible. Healthy individuals gain their edge by learning to balance the two harmoniously.

On the other hand, many athletes prefer not to think of anything while performing. They claim that paying attention to the mechanics of their movements gets in the way. To the extent that actions have become automatic, self-consciousness does indeed impede the free flow of their efforts. They believe it is better to trust their unconscious habits without monitoring every step of their performance. Along these lines, I can't help thinking about the centipede in the Russian children's story who, after being asked what his forty-seventh leg did when his twenty-first moved forward, started to think about it and then could not walk at all!

Although we developed a number of different methods at our Moscow labs for helping our athlete clients achieve heightened performance, the most effective was the process we called auto-conditioning training, ACT.

EXERCISES

Auto-Conditioning Training (ACT)

Each step described here must be mastered before going on to the next. Results can be achieved only if you carefully follow the instructions and *exercise every day*. Don't become discouraged if you don't achieve the desired results right away. ACT has a gradual, cumulative effect.

In auto-conditioning training, you will learn how to place yourself in a relaxed, receptive state, where your entire being will be ready to receive self-suggestions that can be used to enhance your emotional well-being and sharpen your performance.

Researchers at Leipzig University in East Germany have observed that the cadences of baroque music tend to synchronize with various rhythms of the body, from heartbeat to brain waves. They recommend accompanying ACT sessions with slow movements from Bach or Vivaldi concertos, for instance. At the Institute, we never worked with our athletes without playing a suitable audio tape in the background to create a receptive mood.

The following procedure lets your words work for you by means of auto-conditioning, or self-hypnosis, as it is known in the West. In order to use this principle to empower your own words and produce changes in body, emotions, and thoughts, you must believe that they are true (that is, that they represent reality correctly).

Start by trying to produce the feeling of *warmth* in your hands. In the morning, after you finish your shower, step outside the stream of water, then adjust it to considerably warmer. Close your eyes and squeeze your right index finger with your left hand, while saying the word *on*. After that, place both hands under the warm stream of water, and repeat to yourself five times, "**My hands are becoming warmer**."

After you finish this procedure, remove your hands from the water, squeeze your left index finger with your right hand, and say the word *off*.

By pairing physical sensations (warmth) with your words, you establish a mental connection between them. The new habit that you are forming by squeezing your right finger serves as a triggering factor to empower your words, making them not just words but reality itself. We use the right finger because the right hand has its representation in the left-brain (verbal) hemisphere.

Next, conduct a similar procedure designed to envoke a feeling of *heaviness* in your arm. Lie down on your back and place some heavy object on your right arm (it can be a pillow with a couple of thick books on it). Close your eyes, squeeze your right index finger, and say slowly five times: *on*.

Next, repeat slowly five times: "**My arm is becoming heavy**."

Finally, squeeze your left index finger while saying the word *off*. Then remove the weight from your arm.

Do these two exercises for fifteen minutes every night for at least five consecutive days before moving on to the next step.

Entering the Auto-Conditioning State (ACS)

Lie down in a place that will be free from interruption or distraction. (After you master ACT, it will not matter where or under what circumstances you practice it. You will be able to use it while at your desk, riding on the bus, or preparing for a game in a crowded locker room.) Disconnect the telephone. Leave a soft light on and loosen any clothing that may be too tight—belt, shoes, tie, shirt buttons. In fact, you may be most comfortable without any clothing at all.

As with the preliminary exercise, have a tape recorder set up with appropriate music playing. With your head slightly pillowed and eyes closed, let your arms rest alongside your body, palms down, and keep your legs straight. You are about to produce two main symptoms of physical relaxation—feelings of heaviness and warmth in your body.

Squeezing your right index finger, while saying the word *on*.

The first step for inducing *ACS* is relaxation of your muscles. Repeat yourself slowly: "**I am becoming *quiet and relaxed*.**" As you say the first two words, inhale; as you say the words *quiet and relaxed*, exhale. This pairs the sensation of relaxation you experience when you exhale with the key words of your phrase. Now repeat the phrase again. Note that the pause after each phrase should be twice as long as the phrase itself. (In other words, the pause should take two breaths, during which you do not repeat the phrase again. What you should do during the pause is to visualize and try to experience what you have just said to yourself.)

Exhale on the words *quiet and relaxed*, and repeat the phrase three more times.

After repeating the first phrase, visualize during the pause that you are breathing out the tension from your body. You can imagine the tension as a black cloud that you collect from your body while inhaling, and that you then blow out while exhaling.

Now imagine your attention as a beam of light, emanating from your forehead. You are in complete control of this beam; you can direct it anywhere you choose.

For the next phrase, place the focus of your attention into your right arm and say to yourself, "**My arm is** ***becoming heavy***." Repeat this phrase three more times, remembering to take the pauses between the repetitions. During the pauses, visualize the weight pressing down on your arm. Feel your arm as heavy as a piece of lead.

Next, tell yourself, "**My arm is** ***heavy and warm***" (repeat four times). Use your conditioning from the preliminary exercise and imagine your arm under the stream of warm water from your shower. Feel a pleasurable heaviness flow into your arm, along with a soothing warmth. Feel your arm expanding, becoming bigger, swollen with warmth.

"**Both arms are** ***heavy and warm***" (repeat four times).

Now, direct your attention to your face and say, "**My forehead is** ***smoothing out***" (repeat three times). Feel your forehead relaxing, as if someone were gently pulling your skin upward and all lines and tension wrinkles were smoothed away.

Next: "**My eyes are** ***becoming motionless***" (repeat twice). Feel your eyes relaxing, just staring into white nothingness.

"**My lips are** ***relaxing***" (repeat twice). Feel your cheeks become soft and your lips gently part.

"**My jaws are** ***becoming loose***" (repeat twice). Let your jaw hang loose with your mouth half-opened. Now feel your whole face become quiet and motionless like a mask.

"**My neck is** ***relaxing***" (repeat three times). Let the muscles in your neck become softer and warmer. Feel the weight of your head supported by the pillow. Imagine the tension in your muscles as crystals of ice that begin to melt as they become warmer.

"**My shoulders are *sagging***" (repeat twice). This process starts with the muscles of your neck.

"**My back is *relaxing***" (repeat three times). Now the ice crystals in your muscles are beginning to melt along your back and spine. Your whole torso becomes heavier and warmer, its weight supported entirely by the bed.

"**My buttocks are *becoming soft***" (repeat twice). Imagine the ice crystals melting throughout the muscles of your pelvis.

"**My legs are becoming *heavy and warm***" (repeat three times). Feel your thighs, calves, and then your feet melting into delicious, heavy warmth.

"**My stomach is becoming *warm and soft***" (repeat twice). Imagine your stomach muscles slowly melting, as you breathe out all the tension knotted inside.

By this stage your whole body should be utterly relaxed and your muscles free from residual tension. Now that your body is no longer flooding your brain with electrical impulses, your mind should be starting to relax as well. One of the signs of mental relaxation is the feeling of drowsiness. Reinforce the drowsiness by saying: "**I feel *pleasantly drowsy***" (repeat twice).

(One of the dangers of this training is that you may fall asleep without finishing the exercise. Try to become aware of the onset of slumber and fight it by tightening up some of your muscles—clench your teeth or your fists, for example.)

Another sign of mental relaxation is the sensation of time slowing down. Reinforce this by saying: "**Everything is *slowing down***" (repeat twice).

If your mind has a tendency to wander at this point, you can curb it best not by fighting each extraneous thought but by acknowledging its presence and then letting it pass by. You can further quiet your mind by saying: "**I am *resting***" (repeat three times). Now relaxation permeates every pore of your body, every cell of your brain. Imagine your mind as the quiet surface of a lake . . . All your problems and anxieties slowly dissolve in this lake of serentiy. The purifying waters of the lake spread through your whole being, filling you with peace and tranquility.

Remain in this state for about ten minutes, before ending your session. Then press on your left index finger and say *off*.

You should arise refreshed and in your SOF. Now, you should be able to face whatever challenges are in your path with a level of heightened performance that will far exceed your former capacities.

Spend about one week mastering ACS. Practice it twice a day for at least half an hour in the late afternoon after work, and at night before going to sleep. You can then reduce the number of repetitions of each phrase without losing the effect.

7 TAPPING YOUR CO-PERSONALITIES

Soviet psychologists believe that we all possess multiple personalities, and that, by learning to summon or suppress them at will, we can elicit the most effective aspect for dealing with any situation.

Like their Western counterparts, Russian psychologists believe that people actually use only a fraction of their natural resources. This view is supported by feats of sudden mental superperformance that appear to emerge from some mysterious inner resources of the mind. In the earlier chapters, most of our discussion concerned physical feats of peak performance. In similar fashion, emergency situations can inspire people of average intellect to display astounding insight and shine with unusual creativity. Works of genius have not always been produced by geniuses, although history has preserved their names in its annals alongside those of truly exceptional persons.

Professor Leonid Gissen, my mentor at the Moscow Institute, used to illustrate this point with the following anecdote from French history.

In Paris, in the year 1789, lived a man called Rouget de Lisle, an amateur musician and rather mediocre poet—hardly a luminary in a nation that had been fostering great talents as long as it had existed. It was a time of turmoil, and all around Rouget, revolution was in the air. On July 14, the predicted revolt of the masses against Louis XVI and Marie Antoinette suddenly erupted.

Rouget de Lisle found himself in the midst of an open conflict: armed men and women dashed by, ready to face a decisive fight with the reactionary regime. The air itself crackled with agitation. As he witnessed history taking place before his eyes, the thrill of it all penetrated right to the core of Rouget's soul. Riding this wave of patriotic fervor, infused with excitement, he sat down under a tree and jotted down some words to the strange, emotion-filled rhythm permeating his whole being: "Forward, children of the fatherland." The voice inside him grew stronger as he feverishly continued: "The day of glory has arrived!" Within twenty minutes, he had completed the song. The famous "Marseillaise" would become the musical emblem of the French Revolution and later—to this day—the country's national anthem.

Rouget never created anything of value after that, reverting to his previous state of mediocrity.

MULTIPLE SELVES

How do Russian psychologists interpret such sporadic peak performance? The Soviets subscribe to the theory that human beings are composed of a multitude of different facets, or *co-personalities*. This theory was originally formulated by the brilliant Russian philosopher, Gurdjieff, born in 1877 in Alexandropol. Gurdjieff emigrated to Paris not long after the Communist revolution, like so many Russian luminaries of the time. Since then, the Soviets have deleted his name from psychology textbooks, but his theories continue to appear, albeit anonymously. Quick as the Soviet government may be to pounce on brilliant research and development, it gives actual credit only to those who have unrelentingly dedicated their work to the betterment of the Communist state.

Gurdjieff's concept of the multiple self is enthusiastically endorsed by some prominent Soviet psychologists. The so-called Composition Principle is based on the idea that each human being—each self—is not a totality, an indivisible unity, but rahter an unlimited number of different facets. And, as a corollary conclusion to this principle, the more facets of yourself you know and use, the better your performance. The *samorazvitie* movement is built on the principle that to make gifted individuals useful to the state, their best characteristics must be brought out and their less desirable ones suppressed.

For a visual analogy, we can compare the human mind to a multifaceted crystal, some of whose planes are lit up and plainly visible, while other facets are buried in darkness (the unconscious). For example, what I call "I" (Grigori Raiport) consists in fact of many different selves, each pressing for action. These separate selves are not roles but psychological realities: child, leader, coward, martyr. Let's call them "co-personalities" or "co-pers."

The following Tibetan analogy exemplifies the Russian concept of the individual:

> A person is an assembly composed of a number of members. In this assembly discussions never cease. Now and again one of the members rises, makes a speech,

> and suggests an action; his colleagues approve, and it is decided that what he proposed will be executed. Often several members of the assembly rise at the same time and propose different things.

STRENGTHENING YOUR POSITIVE SELVES

Because it is impossible to concentrate on two things at the same time, only a single, strong co-personality can occupy center stage at any given time. What allows one particular co-personality to jump to the forefront of your being and be granted its moment of power? The fact is, each of your several personalities emerges from a specific situation or triggering factor. Your "killer" co-pers, for example, will appear during a life-threatening circumstance that demands the most drastic measures of self-preservation—say, when a mugger holds a gun against your belly. Or if you are a woman, your "mother" co-pers might be triggered by the appearance of a lost and helpless toddler in search of its parent.

Each human being is endowed with dormant co-personalities who may or may not ever be called to action. Some of them lie waiting only for the right conditions to emerge. Once in Moscow, ten-year-old Olga K. was brought to me. Her parents felt that she possessed a natural predilection for dance. But before allowing her to audition for the Bolshoi School of Ballet, which trains young dancers for many years before incorporating them into the company, her mother wanted Olga tested at the Institute.

Sure enough, Olga was limber and strong, capable of enduring long periods of physical strain. She was eager to become a dancer, and her self-image as such was already well defined. We spoke of her concept of herself as a ballerina, and I took her to a number of dress rehearsals at the Bolshoi to watch her reaction as she became steeped in the atmosphere of the company and the hall. It was fascinating to observe this unformed child reveal her seedling self, her "ballerina" co-personality, which needed only to be trained and guided. Yes, I reported, this child indeed possessed all the prerequisites for auditioning for the Bolshoi School's admission committee.

I continued to work with Olga after she was accepted at the school. Twice a week, I practiced psychological techniques to evoke and strengthen her "ballerina" co-pers, while pushing aside some other selves that were getting in the way of her study of ballet. Through auto-conditioning training, Olga learned to "put to sleep" the irresponsible co-pers (we all have one) who tended to disrupt her concentration. We also weakened her "glutton" co-pers, because a dancer must remain slender. Her "mischievous child" co-pers was allowed ample room, however, since a ten-year-old has to let off steam and act out her need for fun, games, and pranks.

THE HIERARCHY OF PERSONALITIES

Lack of understanding of the multiplicity of human nature often leads to common misconceptions. We often hear phrases like, "Yesterday I just wasn't myself, I was so angry." The fact is that person *was* himself or herself, although the self in this case was one that rarely comes forth. Co-personalities can be classified by the frequency with which they are used.

The first group of co-personalities are those you use *habitually, most of the time* (male, husband, son). The second group are those you experience *occasionally* (enraged child, depressed pessimist). The third group contains those you have experienced *rarely* in your life, under highly unusual circumstances (passionate leader, traitor). The fourth, last group includes those dormant selves you *never* have had occasion to summon forth and of which you may not even be aware (hero, killer, genius, thief).

Take a brief inventory of your own co-personalities by listing all those you are aware of, labeling them according to the frequency of their occurrence in your life.

Write them all down. Take your time.

1. Habitually:
2. Occasionally:
3. Rarely:
4. Never:

For example, if you are a "spouse" *habitually*, a "baseball player" *occasionally*, and a "concerned godparent" *rarely*, you would place these selves in the first, second, and third groups, respectively.

This exercise is designed to map out your co-personalities, for each of us possesses different selves of various strengths. You will discover many of which you had been unaware, and new ones may keep coming to your attention for weeks or even months after doing the exercise.

It's interesting to note that your highest as well as lowest potential selves are hidden in the fourth layer. Why?

Fear of the unknown—those co-personalities you haven't explored yet—may be the only wall separating you from your potential greatness. Self-discovery is often hampered by fear that the genies unleashed from the bottle of your subconscious might take control—with negative or destructive results. The opposite, in fact, is true: the less aware you are of your latent co-personalities, the more power they possess to rule your behavior. The most dangerous enemy is the hidden one (i.e., the one contained by your subconscious).

Your various co-personalities have different levels of maturity as well, for the more often you exercise a given co-pers, the more developed it becomes. Depending on the frequency of use, co-personalities can have different ages of development. In the Herman Hesse novel *Steppenwolf*, Harry is learning to dance. His girl remarks: "In you the spiritual part is very highly developed, and so you are very backward in all the little arts of living. Harry-the-thinker is a hundred years old, but Harry-the-dancer is scarcely half a day old." If you have no occasion to call forth one of your co-personalities, it can remain dormant forever.

In formal logic, if A is A, it cannot also be B. But according to the theory of co-personalities, A *can* be B as well. A human being can be good one moment and evil the next (some of the cruelest Nazi leaders were also devoted husbands and fathers). Pushing this idea one step further, we find that a positive co-pers cannot exist without a negative co-pers, the way the plus of the magnet cannot exist without the minus. No wonder that the other side of sensitivity is vulnerability, and the positive aspect of stubbornness is persistence.

Soviet psychologists recognize the advantage of bringing forth any latent co-pers, no matter how negative it may seem to the individual concerned. They believe that every co-pers possesses energy, which, if properly channeled, can be used constructively. Not only can a human being be both good and evil, but often a particular quality, pushed to its extreme, can change into its opposite. For example, kindness, when pushed to its extreme, turns into a negative attribute. Imagine an extremely kind judge who lets a criminal loose. In this case, kindness turns into a vice.

One of my clients, Dina C., was well respected by her friends and colleagues for her orderly habits and well-organized mind. At home, however, Dina was possessed by a compulsion for neatness that made life virtually impossible for her family. It seems that one's minuses are a continuation of one's pluses . . . and vice versa.

MAKING USE OF YOUR UNDESIRABLE SELVES

This leads us to a theory called *psychological relativism*: no human characteristic is absolutely good or absolutely bad. It can be good or bad in relation to a given circumstance. Take, for instance, a "killer" co-pers. Is it good or bad? Well, if you kill enemies during a war you may win a medal, but if you kill someone in the course of committing robbery, you will deserve a long jail sentence. It becomes obvious, therefore, that co-personalities are morally neutral.

In Rostov, for example, I once worked with a local runner, Sergei Mladin, who complained of lack of competitiveness. During our sessions, I discovered that his main co-pers was "Destructive Sergei," who would smash the china on the table if his wife upset him, or beat his dog if it misbehaved. Generally he was a kind and loving person, and Sergei was quite ashamed to accept this side of himself. He fought against it for a long time.

To Sergei's surprise, I did not suggest performing radical surgery on this unattractive co-pers. Instead I encouraged him to harness it to help his running. Obviously, "Destructive Sergei" could not be allowed to continue being harmful, but charged as it was with energy, it could be used positively. I therefore taught Sergei to rename this dominant co-pers "Competitive Sergei" and encouraged him to direct its expression toward outrunning his competitors rather than wreaking violence on his family. In general, one can gain control over one's co-pers through the process of disidentification (described later in this chapter).

It often pays to discover one's dormant co-pers, as my chess champion friend Lev Alburt came to realize. After leaving the USSR for good, he perfected his English and went on to become the U.S. chess champion. As we became better acquainted in New York, I saw that Lev possessed a rare gift for oration and writing, along with a strong passion for politics.

Why not capitalize on being U.S. champion, I suggested, and start writing articles and delivering lectures that would help inform the public about how the Soviets use chess strategies—such as thinking at least three moves ahead of one's opponent—to achieve a critical edge. Lev demurred. A quiet fellow, he could not see himself in that role. After all, he explained, he was not really a writer. However, he decided to work with me for a few weeks, to see what I could do to help him overcome this natural reticence. We started with the idea that while "chess champion" was a worthwhile co-pers, it need not crowd out other talents he possessed. I proposed imagery exercises to broaden his notion of self, allowing space for his "politician" co-pers to emerge and grow.

With Lev, I did not use the "empty vessel" technique employed with other patients. Instead, we worked on removing the boundaries that he had placed around his idea of self. We imagined Lev's total being as a boundless field full of co-personalities, like seeds waiting to blossom. A month later, he began writing articles and speaking at political conferences. Later he went to work on a book of his thoughts and research on world politics.

Once you learn the extent of your own diversity and understand that your inherent multiplicity gives you a wide range of options, you will be able to select the most appropriate facet of your self for each situation you face. Once you gain awareness of your "dark sides," you can analyze your most dangerous weaknesses and see where they stem from.

In this way, I helped wrestler Anatoly V. summon forth his "killer" co-pers, keeping his gentle, considerate self at bay for a match. And the pianist Vera D. needed to forget her home and family during performances, subjugating her "wife" co-pers to her "performer" co-pers. Neither Anatoly nor Vera had understood that they possessed a conflicting set of co-personalities that prevented peak performance.

Most people exercise very little control over their multiple selves, allowing them to be activated according to the stimulus-response principle. Because a specific situation tends to trigger an appropriate co-pers, it is tempting to shift responsibility to that external situation, rather than to admit that the emergence of a given co-pers can ultimately be a matter of personal choice. What are the factors that bring to life one's various selves?

At the Institute, we dealt with a lot of issues having to do with co-personalities, for top athletes need to strengthen specific ones in order to become habitual winners. We explained to our clients that we were not denying their other selves, but rather we were teaching them to elicit only the self that would allow them to achieve their SOF. In order to do so, each individual was asked to isolate the particular trigger factors bringing on the co-pers in question. Different triggers produce different co-personalities. With hunger may come a "glutton" co-personality, while the gentle sounds of soft music may bring out a "sentimental" self, and so on.

We also discovered that other people can become triggers. When I was around my mentor, Leonid Gissen, his wisdom tended to evoke my own "wiseman" co-pers, while with my friend Sonya, who was younger and more vulnerable than I, my "older brother" co-pers had a chance to emerge. With Vladimir, I can be foolish and childlike; he evokes my "prankster" co-pers. My psychiatrist friend Anatoly brings to life my "introspective" self.

If you would like to know which of your co-personalities your friends appeal to, do the following. Write down the names of your five closest friends and, alongside each name, which co-pers this person tends to bring to light. You will probably find that one friend may elicit several different co-personalities in you.

As a rule, the closeness of relationships is in direct ratio to the number of co-personalities two people share. Just as we choose the professional and service people who satisfy our various needs—a housekeeper to clean, an accountant to prepare our tax forms—so we tend to select our friends to satisfy our various selves. Usually, spouses or lovers bring out a great variety of co-personalities in each other. It is not true that opposites attract, as popular wisdom has it. Maybe they do in the beginning, but they surely don't stay together for long. Usually the more facets and interests you have in common with your mate, the more solid the relationship.

THE DOMINANTA PRINCIPLE

Although modern Soviet psychology has been influenced by Gurdjieff's ideas, no Russian has affected the field as profoundly as Ivan Pavlov, with his emphasis on physiological laws of the human mind. It was Pavlov's fundamental belief that behavior, once reinforced, would perpetuate itself, becoming second nature. In his experiments with dogs, he proved conclusively that one could train an animal—and, by extension, a human being—to respond predictably to a given stimulus. His student A. A. Ukhtomsky pushed this motion one important step further, his Dominanta Principle incorporating Pavlov's ideas with those of Gurdjieff.

Ukhtomsky discovered that when one area of the cortex of the brain is excited, it tends to suppress the activity of all other areas, enabling one emotion (or idea) to become the single force ruling a person's behavior. He proved that once one co-personality occupies mental space, it tends to push aside and dominate all others. Contemporary Soviet psychologist P. K. Anokhin remarks that "when Dominanta emerges, it suppresses in the central nervous system all other 'functional systems' [another term for co-pers]."

If one Dominanta persists, it can crystallize into the very character of a person, attaining the power of compulsiveness. My best friend in Russia was the national long-jump champion, Vladimir Skibyenko. As a child,

Vladimir had suffered mental abuse from his father, who called him *samocer* ("one who eats dung"). This word is used in Russian to describe a perennial loser who cannot help but create disaster all around him. In spite of this, Vladimir became not only a successful doctor but also an award-winning athlete. His self-image, however, was low enough to cause him serious problems during some crucial competitions, and he came to me for assistance.

I realized that the Dominanta Principle was involved: my friend's "*samocer*" co-pers had crystallized into his dominant self. Since we did much work with imagery in Russia, I sat down with Vladimir and told him to imagine his "I"—his self—as an empty vessel waiting to be filled by the waters of his various co-personalities.

"Visualize each co-pers as having a particular color," I continued. "These colors can mix together. If your 'winner' co-pers is red, and your '*samocer*' co-pers is blue, your self will contain a purplish sort of water. Now visualize the hose that pours the blue water in as being full of holes. Feel the water seep out of the hose before it's emptied into the vessel of your self, while the red water of your 'winner' co-pers flows in strongly and steadily. As your self becomes filled with red water, only a little of the blue penetrates. Feel that self growing stronger, more confident, triumphant, as the red water drowns out the blue. And now the vessel is full and no more blue water can pour in at all."

I worked with Vladimir in this way every week for three months, weakening his negative "*samocer*" while strengthening his "winner" co-pers. Gradually the pattern of his dominant co-personality changed. As everyone knows who has had the pleasure of watching him perform, Vladimir went on to new heights in his athletic career.

EXERCISE

Personality Modification

You can also use the disidentification technique to enhance and strengthen desirable areas of your personality. This prodecure consists of three steps: minimizing your negative co-personalities, maximizing your positive ones, and action reinforcement.

1. DETECT AND MINIMIZE YOUR NEGATIVE IDENTIFICATIONS. What are your negative identities? Write down a list of your dominant negative co-personalities, those that rule your behavior the most often. They can be anything: loser, coward, victim, frustrated romantic, complainer, Jewish mama. Now give each one of them an image: your co-pers can look like a rock, an animal, a human being.

Now get into the auto-conditioning state (ACS) and recite to yourself:

"**I have a 'loser' co-pers, but *I am not a loser*.**" Visualize your co-pers inside your head. See it melting down and evaporating with every exhalation.

Repeat the same procedure for every negative co-pers.

2. DETECT AND MAXIMIZE YOUR POSITIVE CO-PERSONALITIES. Take a look at your Target-Self list (Chapter 2). Mark desirable qualities you would like to develop. Now translate them into co-personalities. Take courage, for example. The corresponding co-pers would be "Brave John" or "Brave Joan" (use your name, of course). Give it a shape. Recite the phrase: "**I am *'Brave John.'*** "

Visualize a situation that requires courage: an encounter with your boss, asking a friend for a favor, or fighting off your neighbor's dog. Visualize your brave co-pers as it fuses intimately with your center.

Become aware of the particular emotion that the image elicits. Stay with it for a while and give it a color. Imagine a chest of drawers in your solar plexus (we tend to store our feelings there), and store this emotion in one of the empty drawers. Now you can call on it when you wish.

3. ACTION REINFORCEMENT. Create a situation in your life in which you can exercise your courage. Let it be something simple. If you experience fear of dealing with your boss or another colleague, start with the colleague. Try to choose a no-lose situation—for example, when you are clearly right in an argument. Recite to yourself the phrase, "**I am 'Brave John,'** " and summon the accompanying emotion. Now you are ready for confrontation!

After you win an argument, congratulate yourself for victory by being aware of your feelings of pride and self-respect. Remember that even a small victory makes you much stronger.

8 IDENTIFYING WITH YOUR WINNING SELF

Russian performance experts believe that overidentification with our less desirable traits can hinder the development of more desirable qualities.

Sometimes in order to achieve the mental and emotional freedom necessary to become the best you can be, it is essential to clear your inner core of any and all co-personalities. Only then is it possible to discover your true center of identity, what I call your "winning self."

Over the years, Soviet psychologists have evolved a technique for achieving this goal. They call it *disidentification*. Disidentification is a kind of mental purge that leaves you free to discover the infinite possibilities at your disposal. Through disidentification you come to realize that while you may possess any number of co-personalities, you do not have to be bound by any of them.

IDENTITY

I was jaywalking on Gorki Street in Moscow, lost in thought, when the sharp whistle of a militiaman in a red cap rudely interrupted the meanderings of my speculations.

"Your identification, please," he demanded, his pasted-on smile promising me a ticket. I handed over my passport, which told the vigilant militiaman that my name was Grigori Raiport and that I was a male citizen of the USSR, a physician, and twenty-eight years of age. My Muscovite nemesis duly noted all these facts and handed me the expected ticket. As far as he was concerned, he knew all about me.

However, while the various attributes of Grigori Raiport evident to that militiaman were all part of my identity, not one was my true identity. They were all merely the externals, tags that other people used to label me. A problem develops when we begin to identify ourselves too intimately with one of these attributes, letting it dominate the others. This *pseudoidentity*, as Soviet psychologists call it, can leach space away from other, often more meaningful aspects of the self, stunting the depth and range of internal growth while throwing the whole personality out of balance. Such a situation is bound to affect performance and hinder success.

Psychologists call the process by which we grow to intimately associate ourselves with some aspect of ourselves *identification*. My Russian mentor Dr. Gissen, who had studied the works of Italian psychologist Roberto Assogiolli, described the two basic principles involved in identification:

PRINCIPAL 1. You are controlled by everything with which you identify yourself.

PRINCIPLE 2. You can control everything from which your disidentify yourself.

The process of disidentification consists of weakening dominant pseudoidentities by creating space between them and your true self. Its goal is to discover your true identity, for only then is it possible to freely choose who you want to be and confidently set out on the path of self-development. In our Moscow lab we achieved this goal through a special exercise, which you will learn to perform at the end of the chapter. This exercise resembles a mental purge that leaves you free to sense the infinite possibilities at your disposal. For though you may possess any number of facets or co-personalities, you are not bound by any single one of them.

I had occasion to put Gissen's method into practice on Olympic gymnast Ludmilla Turischeva, who tended to fall into the trap of identifying herself with her body. If she didn't feel in prime physical condition, Turischeva lost confidence in her ability to win; thus her overidentification with her body was controlling her and impairing her performance. I used a visualization exercise that is as effective as it is unpleasant. First I asked this splendid athlete to recline in a chair and picture herself minus one of her legs, lost in a car accident. "Tell me how you feel, and what you're thinking and doing," I encouraged her.

Her eyes glued shut, Ludmilla took a minute to reply. "Well . . ." She hesitated, scrunching her nose up in initial distaste. "I see myself on crutches, looking down at the ring where my former colleagues are performing. I feel pain, envy, anger. I think that I am going to have to find something to replace gymnastics in my life, and suddenly I'm scared. What if there isn't anything else I can be good at?"

"This all makes perfect sense," I assured her. "But tell me, Ludmilla, who are you now?"

She shook her head, bewildered. "I'm still *me*," she answered, a little annoyed. "I mean . . . leg or no leg, I have the same heart, the same morality, the same way of thinking. Of course I'm the same person!"

This realization proved to be a turning point in Turischeva's development as an athlete. Once she was able to understand that she, her mental self, was far more than her physical body, she was able to perform with greater confidence, whether she felt in top physical condition or not. This provided an edge that led to many victories on days when she would otherwise have given up.

Another example of how disidentification can liberate us from unwanted pseudoidentities involved Raisa T., a soccer player I worked with at the Institute. Raisa had a problem controlling her anger. When things didn't go well on the playing field, she would become so enraged she could no longer perform at her peak.

One evening when they had just ordered dinner at a restaurant, Raisa's boyfriend Ivan decided he wanted some beer. "I thought he was just going to order a bottle from the bar," she recounted. "But instead, he left the restaurant. I waited five, ten, fifteen minutes. Our food arrived and I was sitting there like a total fool, feeling abandoned and humiliated in front of everyone. How dare Ivan do this to me?"

Upset and agitated, Raisa went out into the street and encountered Ivan approaching with a six-pack in a brown paper bag. "I threw myself at him like a crazy person, grabbed his bag, and hurled the pack into the street, where jets of beer began to explode out of the punctured cans. Then I happened to catch my reflection in a shop window. The view shocked me: shaking, my face haggard with rage, I was actually foaming at the mouth. This image produced a sobering effect on me. I realized I had made myself look like a fool with my angry tirade and accomplished absolutely nothing. I got a grip on my rage. I simply told Ivan that his behavior had been unacceptable, said a calm and cold good night, then took the next bus home."

Raisa's glimpse of her own contorted face reflected in the window caused her to regain her self-control. Once she was able to see her anger objectively, from the outside, she realized it was not really an inseparable part of her personality after all. This helped her to dissociate from her anger; she was able to control it instead of letting it control her, and her soccer performance remained at a consistently high level, no matter what emotional provocation she received.

PSEUDOIDENTITY

What are some of the common pseudoidentities that fuse with people's true selves? Sometimes people identify themselves with their country, thereby feeling inseparable from it, unable to imagine living without it. When their country appeals to them to die defending it in what may be a dubious war, they often say they feel compelled to heed the call, never realizing how controlled they are by the mere fact of the identification. Other people are controlled by and identify with their material possessions ("Who are you?" "I am a millionaire.").

Paul, a friend of mine, had saved for years to buy his dream house. Finally his day of triumph came: he became the proud owner of a monumental two-story construction, right on the ocean in Malibu, California. Paul identified himself with his spectacular home. When the house was praised, *he* felt praised; when the house was criticized, *he* felt criticized.

One day, a storm damaged one of the Doric columns outside the imposing entrance of the house. Paul became greatly disturbed. He felt the house and himself damaged, unpresentable. Unwilling to let his friends view his other "self" in such a condition, Paul moved his long-planned birthday party from the house to a nearby banquet hall, at far greater expense.

People also tend to identify themselves with their children or spouses, so that a child's success is their success, or a spouse's failure their failure. Investing one's identity in others can be a dangerous practice; one surrenders possession of one's very self.

Still others identify themselves with their appearance, especially actors or models who earn their living through their beauty. When age starts to creep up, and wrinkles begin to undermine the flawless exterior, they start to panic.

One of my patients at the Moscow Institute, a world-class chess player, was a magnetic, exciting woman in her thirties. Irina was elegant, stylish, and had an interesting, exotic face. All her life, men had told her that she was attractive, and she identified herself with this quality.

Then Irina married a terribly handsome man. From the first moment of their marriage, he was unfaithful. Later, Irina told me she had asked him why he desired other women: "He thinks I'm ugly, and that he deserves a more beautiful partner." This caused Irina to go into a tailspin and lose confidence in every area of her life, including her ability to play chess. Once Irina felt stripped of her attractiveness, she felt stripped of her identity as well.

At our first consultation, Irina had the vacant, frightened look of a lost child. Where was her sense of self? Clearly, she had always carried an erroneous idea of who Irina truly was, allowing a pseudoidentity to take over her mental and emotional life until she no longer realized she had any other attributes to draw upon. In order to help her, I taught her a simple technique for dissociating herself from this domineering identification.

I had Irina memorize the phrase, "I possess beauty, but I am not my beauty." I encouraged her to imagine herself separating from her face and hair and standing back a pace. She learned to internalize this image, and to understand that what had made her an attractive person in the first place had to do with her total personality and not merely her physical appearance.

In a similar fashion, people—athletes, bodybuilders, actors, dancers—sometimes falsely identify themselves too closely with their bodies. If you ask such persons "How are you?" they will often respond in terms of various bodily sensations: "I'm fine; my biceps gained half an inch, though this tendon I pulled in my knee last Tuesday still bothers me." Many prominent athletes with whom I worked were plunged into depression when they began to lose their agility and were forced into retirement.

Others misidentify themselves with their emotions and feelings. To the question "How are you?" such a person will respond in terms of emotions: "I feel great," or "I'm so excited today!" Often these people will find themselves blindly following pleasurable sensations without any regard for consequences.

Many people erroneously believe that their moods are caused by external factors, such as the weather or the actions of others. Not true. It's your thoughts that produce different emotions. Let's say you come to work and a colleague walks by, saying "Hi." If you think the greeting is sincere, you will feel pleased, in a good mood. But if you think it somewhat cold or sarcastic, then you will feel upset, humiliated, insulted. Thus, it is not the situation itself that causes your mood, but your interpretation of it. Therefore, if you learn to control your thoughts, you will know how to control your moods.

Many intellectuals tend to identify themselves with their thoughts. The trend was created by René Descartes, who proclaimed his famous "I think, therefore I am." But if you observe your own thought process, you will notice that your intellect functions pretty much as a computer—you can observe your various thoughts, judge them, discard one, and summon others—apart from yourself. In this way, you are not in fact your thoughts, although they may be a part of you.

EXERCISES

Disidentification

Disidentification is a process that allows you to distance yourself from your various physical and mental attributes. It allows you to find your true center of identity (i.e., your consciousness), from which you can observe and regulate your various faculties.

That's all there is to it.

Find some quiet place and lie down on your back. After getting yourself in the auto-conditioning state (Chapter 6), recite to yourself the following phrases. Repeat each phrase three times, visualizing it as fully and vividly as possible, exhaling on the italicized part of the phrase. (Make a two-breaths-long pause after each repetition.)

"**I have possessions but *I am not my possessions*.**" Visualize yourself looking at all your possessions: house, car, clothes, and so on, and experience your separateness from all these material accoutrements.

"**I have a body but *I am not my body*.**" Visualize yourself stepping outside your body, looking at it from without, realizing that what you call "self" is different from your body.

"**I have thoughts but *I am not my thoughts*.**" Imagine your thoughts as butterflies, flying around your mental space. Become aware how easily they come and go, while your observing self remains the same.

"**I have emotions but *I am not my emotions*.**"

Creating Your Winning Self

Now visualize yourself lying on a deserted beach. You hear the pleasant sound of the waves; you feel the warm sun on your skin. Suddenly, you notice a narrow shaft of light emanating from the sun. It is slowly descending on you, reaching your forehead. You can feel the warmth-giving ray on your forehead. This beam is filled with vibrant, vivifying energy.

This energy becomes absorbed by your forehead, penetrating deeper, collecting inside, forming a ball of incandescent light. Now, clearly feel this ball of energy right inside your forehead. This ball of light represents your consciousness (i.e., your center of identity).

Now, identify yourself with the ball of light (call it "my center"). Picture your self located inside the ball of light, observing from it everything happening around you.

Recite the following phrase twice: "**I affirm my identity as *my center.* From my center *I can control my body*.**" Visualize your center shooting out beams of light, which reach all parts of your body (arms, legs, heart, etc.). These beams transmit the commnads of your center to the various parts of your body.

Now say: "**From my center *I choose and control my thoughts*.**" Visualize your mental space as large as the room. At the top of the room is your center, a shining ball of light, from which you observe everything that is going on. The room is filled with butterflies—your thoughts. They are diverse and mobile, of different colors. Your center is able to shoot out a beam of light and direct it at any butterfly (i.e., any thought). The beam of light works like a leash; it can pull the captured butterfly closer to your center, so that you can examine the thought in greater detail. And you can keep the thought on your "leash of light" for as long as you want.

"**From my center** ***I choose and control my moods.***" Visualize your moods being stored in the imaginary chest of drawers located in your solar plexus. Imagine that each of your moods sets within its own drawer. The drawers are of different colors. Now, choose the colors of your emotions. What color is happiness for you? What about sadness? Irritability? Aggression? Label each with its own color.

You may wonder how all this can be used to choose and control your moods. The procedure is simple. Take victory, for example. Since you know that your thoughts cause your moods, first summon a victorious thought—one of those butterflies. The color of the butterfly should correspond to the color of the victory drawer in your solar plexus.

Let's say my color for victory is yellow. So I shoot out the beam of light from my center to my yellow victory butterfly. Here it is, right in front of my center, whispering the things I have "won at" in my life. The butterfly can start with those things I usually take for granted, such as "I earn a living. I am good at softball. I'm terrific at barbecuing."

After a few minutes of this "victory report," your yellow butterfly flutters down to your solar plexus and finds a yellow drawer, containing your victorious mood. The butterfly pulls the drawer open and . . . ah! A golden vapor rushes out from the drawer, spreading all over your mind and body, filling you with a victorious feeling. The moment the vapor pours out of the drawer, the yellow butterfly dissolves in it, symbolizing the fusion of thought with feeling.

The same method works for curtailing negative moods. You feel irritable and want to get rid of your irritability. Let's say that, for you, the color of irritability is gray. The first step is to summon your gray butterfly to your center and let it make an "irritability report" (i.e., all the reasons why you are irritable today).

After the report is over, the gray butterfly slides down to your solar plexus and finds the gray drawer. But what is this? The drawer is already slightly open and the gray vapor of irritability is streaming outside, polluting your mental atmosphere. The gray butterfly squeezes itself into the open space and shuts the drawer from the inside, thereby locking itself inside as well.

PART 2

The Soviet Auto-Conditioning Training Course

1. Preparatory Steps*

As I lead you through the labyrinths of the auto-conditioning course, only one thing is required of you: consistency. Each step described here must be mastered before going on to the next. Results can be achieved only if you carefully follow the instructions and *exercise every day*.

There is a parallel between developing your physical and mental qualities: both require a systematic approach and neither occurs instantaneously. It takes several months to build up your physical fitness; the same amount of time may be required to build up your mental fitness. Don't become discouraged if you don't achieve the desired results right away. Auto-conditioning training (ACT) has a gradual, cumulative effect.

In ACT, you will be learning how to place yourself in a relaxed, receptive state, where your subconscious mind will be ready to receive self-suggestions such as "I am feeling at my optimum" or "I will wake up with the solution to my problem in mind" that can be used to enhance your emotional well-being and sharpen your performance.

MAKING GANZ-FIELD GOGGLES

Start by making yourself "ganz-field" (total field) goggles. German psychologists have discovered that exposing the

*You can order the ACT training kit by writing to Russian Success Method, 250 W. 57th St., # 1527, New York, NY 10107.

retina to a completely white field for a time can synchronize brain waves, creating a trance-like state in which the individual feels relaxed and receptive.

To make the goggles, all you need are two table-tennis balls. Cut them in half with small scissors. Discard the halves with a label mark on them. File the edges of the remaining halves—your goggles—in order not to scratch your skin.

To put on the goggles, lie on your back in a lighted room. With your thumb on your cheekbone and your index finger beneath your brow, gently pull the skin around your eyes apart. Now install the goggles. Keep your eyes open.

It's all right to blink or move your eyes, though the latter is not recommended; just stare into the white nothingness. In about ten minutes, you should start observing some interesting effects: you may not be aware of whether your eyes are open or closed; your thoughts may become fragmented and elusive; and you may experience a slight state of drowsiness. You may also see some fleeting images and sporadic colors. The effect is called blank-out.

After you repeat this experience two or three times, you can proceed to the next step.

2. Attention-Control Exercises

The following exercises have two goals. First, they prepare you for ACT. In ACT you are supposed to direct your attention to different parts of your body: first the left arm, then the right, then the neck, and then the muscles; attention also plays an important part in the imagery aspect of ACT, where you imagine your thoughts taking different forms or envision your ideal self. Second, these exercises have value in themselves, because the ability to control your attention is crucial in any performance—athletic, professional, artistic. For example, the ability to direct and control your attention will help you prevent self-defeating thoughts that could affect your presentation or performance.

SWITCHING ATTENTION

The objective of this exercise is to train you to switch your attention at will and maintain it for a prolonged period of time.

- Get two radios. Place one about five feet to your left and another the same distance to your right. Tune to two different stations and adjust the volumes equally to a pleasant, moderate level.
- Sit between the radios with your eyes closed. Visualize your attention as a beam of light emanating from your forehead. Alternate your attention back

and forth every twenty seconds from one radio to the other by snapping your fingers. Do this exercise five minutes daily until you reach the goal of being able to concentrate totally on one station while "tuning out" the other.

- Read a book while the news is on the radio. Alternate your attention for about twenty seconds each between reading and listening, and then try to become oblivious to what you are reading while you are listening, and vice versa. Do this for at least five minutes every day until you reach your objective: total concentration on reading to the total exclusion of the news.
- Learn to become an introvert at will. Imagine turning the beam of your attention inward. While the news is still on the radio, start subtracting in your mind the number 7 from 100. Do this exercise daily until you can become oblivious to the news while subtracting.

Once you have mastered this exercise, start doing similar things with people. When several people are talking to you at the same time, choose which one to listen to and block out the competing voices.

STRENGTHENING CONCENTRATION

Sit down by yourself in a room and stare at the second hand of your watch for one minute. See how long you can maintain the following thought: "I am sitting here looking at the hand of the watch." Count how many times your mind veers off from this thought. Repeat this exercise for five minutes every day until you are able to keep your mind completely on this single thought.

SUMMONING AND MANIPULATING IMAGES

The objective of the following exercises is to develop your ability to summon and manipulate images at will. This in turn helps to develop your concentration and patience.

- Choose some simple object—say, a paper clip. Place this paper clip in the center of a white sheet of paper. Study it meticulously for about three minutes, as if you had never seen anything like it before. Pay attention to its form, texture, and color, trying to absorb in your memory as many details as possible.
- Close your eyes and try to visualize the paper clip for about twenty seconds. The image you get will probably be fuzzy and transitory; usually it will move from the right side to the left. Open your eyes and compare your image with the actual paper clip; notice which of its details your image was missing. Remember that whatever evaded your memory must have evaded your perception as well.
- Now close your eyes again and try to reconstruct the image with the new details you've noticed. Open your eyes and again retrace details your image was missing this time. Close your eyes once more, and repeat the whole procedure. Do this for about five minutes each day until you have reached

your goal, which is to keep a sharp and stable image of the paper clip in your mind's eye for at least twenty seconds.

- Develop your objective imagination by learning to manipulate your images. Study an irregular piece of paper from different angles, then close your eyes and start rotating its image in your mind. How does it look from the side? From the top?
- There are two types of imagination: objective and subjective. An example of *objective imagination* would be to visualize a forest by seeing it from the outside with your mind's eye. But if you were to imagine yourself walking in this forest, feeling the grass under your feet, smelling the flowers, that would be *subjective imagination*, for you would be a participant in your image.

With this in mind, close your eyes and visualize your paper clip in a stationary position. Then imagine yourself rotating around it, looking at it from various angles. At first, move around it slowly, taking in every detail; then increase the speed, until you begin feeling a bit dizzy.

PRODUCING BODY CHANGES

The following exercise is designed to use the power of your imagination to produce actual physiological changes in your body.

Place your right index finger on a sheet of paper. Repeat the procedure you followed when you first contemplated the paper clip (study the details of your fingers, then close your eyes and try to see it, and so on). The only difference in this finger exercise is in regard to the location of your image. Whereas the image of the paper clip would be somewhere around your head (usually it is a few inches in front of your forehead), the image of your index finger should coincide with the finger itself. When you close your eyes and try to "see" your finger, its image should be inside the finger itself, where it lies on the piece of paper. In the previous exercises you took your paper clip into your consciousness, while with the finger exercise you place the image of your finger into the finger itself (i.e., you bring your consciousness to your finger).

The success of this exercise will manifest itself in various physical sensations in your finger: you may start experiencing pulsation, warmth, needles-and-pins, or itching.

Practice these exercises for *at least* a week, keeping in mind that you must thoroughly master each one before you can allow yourself to progress to the one that follows.

3. Directing Physiological Changes

This procedure is valuable for two reasons: one, it helps reduce stress by relaxing muscles; two, it prepares you to control and direct your entire physiology for enhanced performance. By learning to make simple physiological changes in your body at will, you will be able to command peak performance from yourself in critical situations.

The following procedure lets your words work for you by means of auto-conditioning, or self-hypnosis, as it is known in the West. In order to use this principle to empower your own words and produce changes in body, emotions, and thoughts, you must believe that they are true (that is, that they represent reality correctly).

Start by trying to produce the feeling of *warmth* in your hands. In the morning, after you finish your shower, step outside the stream of water, then adjust it to considerably warmer. Close your eyes and squeeze your right index finger with your left hand, while saying the word *on*. After that, place both your hands under the warm stream of water, and repeat to yourself five times, "**My hands are becoming warmer**."

After you finish this procedure, remove your hands from the water, squeeze your left index finger with your right hand, and say the word *off*.

By pairing your physical sensations (warmth) with your words, you establish a mental connection between them. The new habit that you are forming by squeezing your right finger serves as a triggering factor to empower your words, making them not just words but reality itself.

We use the right finger because the right hand has its representation in the left-brain (verbal) hemisphere.

Next, conduct a similar procedure designed to evoke a feeling of *heaviness* in your arm. Lie down on your back and place some heavy object on your right arm (it can be a pillow with a couple of thick books on it). Close your eyes, squeeze your right index finger, and say slowly five times: *on*.

Next, repeat slowly five times: "**My arm is becoming heavy**."

Finally, squeeze your left index finger while saying the word *off*. Then remove the weight from your arm.

Do these two exercise for fifteen minutes every night for at least five consecutive days before moving on to the next step.

4. ACS: The Auto-Conditioning State

The goal of this aspect of ACT is to activate your parasympathetic nervous system by producing more of the hormone noradrenaline in your bloodstream. In the West this is known as *relaxation*, because of its effect on muscle tone. Immersion in ACS requires an utter relaxation of the muscles, thereby reducing the flow of electrical impulses to the brain. When your muscles tighten up, they bombard your cortex with electrical impulses transmitted through nerves, which, in turn, cause tension. Most people are unaware of this constant muscle tension, which they have even when they are asleep. Interestingly enough, it's easier to constrict a muscle than to relax it. This may be explained by the process of evolution. In order to survive, it was more important for our ancestors to be able to mobilize quickly in a dangerous situation than to rest idly.

RELAXING THE BODY

You can be sure that your muscles are deeply relaxed if you experience two major signs of relaxation: a feeling of *heaviness* in your body, and a sensation of *warmth* in your skin. (The latter is due to a dilation of blood vessels, allowing the blood to flow freely to the skin.)

Lie down in a place that will be free from any interruption or distraction. (After you master ACT, it will not matter where or under what circumstances you practice it.

You will be able to use it while at your desk, riding on the bus, or preparing for a game in a crowded locker room.) Disconnect the telephone. Leave a soft light on and loosen any clothing that may be too tight—belt, shoes, tie, shirt buttons. In fact, you may be most comfortable without any clothing at all.

As with the preliminary exercise, have a tape recorder set up with appropriate music playing. With your head slightly pillowed, let your arms rest alongside your body, palms down, and keep your legs straight. Put on your goggles, and take about ten minutes for your eyes to adjust to the ganz-field effect. You are about to produce two main symptoms of physical relaxation—feelings of heaviness and warmth in your body.

Squeeze your right index finger, while saying the word *on.*

The first step for inducing ACS is relaxation of your muscles. Repeat to yourself slowly: "**I am *becoming quiet and relaxed*.**" As you say the first two words, inhale; as you say the words *quiet and relaxed*, exhale. This pairs the sensation of relaxation you experience when you exhale with the key words of your phrase. Now repeat the phrase again. Note that the pause after each phrase should be twice as long as the phrase itself. (In other words, the pause should take two breaths, during which you do not repeat the phrase again. What you should do during the pause is to visualize and try to experience what you have just said to yourself.)

Exhale on the words *quiet and relaxed*, and repeat the same phrase three more times.

For example, after repeating the first phrase, visualize during the pause that you are breathing out the tension from your body. You can imagine the tension as a black cloud that you collect from your body while inhaling, and that you then blow out while exhaling.

Now imagine your attention as a beam of light, emanating from your forehead. You are in complete control of this beam; you can direct it anywhere you choose.

For the next phrase, place the focus of your attention into your right arm and say to yourself, "**My arm is *becoming heavy*.**" Repeat this phrase three more times, remembering to take the pauses between the repetitions. During the pauses, visualize the weight pressing down on your arm. Feel your arm as heavy as a piece of lead.

Next, tell yourself, "**My arm is *heavy and warm***" (repeat four times). Use your conditioning from the preliminary exercise and imagine your arm under the stream of warm water from your shower. Feel a pleasurable heaviness flow into your arm, along with a soothing warmth. Feel your arm expanding, becoming bigger, swollen with warmth.

"**Both arms are *heavy and warm***" (repeat four times).

Now, direct your attention to your face and say, "**My forehead is *smoothing out***" (repeat three times). Feel your forehead relaxing, as if someone were gently pulling your skin upward and all lines and tension wrinkles were smoothed away.

Next: "**My eyes are *becoming motionless***" (repeat twice). Feel your eyes relaxing, just staring into white nothingness.

"**My lips are *relaxing***" (repeat twice). Feel your cheeks become soft and your lips gently part.

"**My jaws are *becoming loose***" (repeat twice). Let your jaw hang loose with your mouth half-opened. Now feel your whole face become quiet and motionless like a mask.

"**My neck is *relaxing***" (repeat three times). Let the muscles in your neck become softer and warmer. Feel the weight of your head supported by the pillow. Imagine the tension in your muscles as crystals of ice that begin to melt as they become warmer.

"**My shoulders are *sagging***" (repeat twice). This process starts with the muscles of your neck.

"**My back is *relaxing***" (repeat three times). Now the ice crystals in your muscles are beginning to melt along your back and spine. Your whole torso becomes heavier and warmer, its weight supported entirely by the bed.

"**My buttocks are *becoming soft***" (repeat twice). Imagine the ice crystals melting throughout the muscles of your pelvis.

"**My legs are becoming *heavy and warm***" (repeat three times). Feel your thighs, calves, and then your feet melting into delicious heavy warmth.

"**My stomach is becoming *warm and soft***" (repeat twice). Imagine your stomach muscles slowly melting, as you breathe out all the tension knotted inside.

RELAXING THE MIND

By this stage your whole body should be utterly relaxed and your muscles free from residual tension. Now that your body is no longer flooding your brain with electrical impulses, your mind should be starting to relax as well. One of the signs of mental relaxation is the feeling of drowsiness. Reinforce the drowsiness by saying: "**I feel *pleasantly drowsy***" (repeat twice).

(One of the dangers of this training is that you may fall asleep without finishing the exercise. Try to become aware of the onset of slumber and fight it by tightening up some of your muscles—clench your teeth or your fists, for example.)

Another sign of mental relaxation is the sensation of time slowing down. Reinforce this by saying: "**Everything is *slowing down***" (repeat twice).

If your mind has a tendency to wander at this point, you can curb it best not by fighting each extraneous thought but by acknowledging its presence and then letting it pass by. You can further quiet your mind by saying: "**I am *resting***" (repeat three times). Now relaxation permeates every pore of your body, every cell of your brain. Imagine your mind as the quiet surface of a lake . . . All your problems and anxieties slowly dissolve in this lake of serenity. The purifying waters of the lake spread through your whole being, filling you with peace and tranquility.

Remain in this state for about ten minutes, before ending your session. Then press on your left index finger and say *off.*

You should arise refreshed and in your SOF. Now, you should be able to face whatever challenges are in your path with a level of heightened performance that will far exceed your former capacities.

Spend about one week mastering ACS. Practice it twice a day for at least half an hour in the late afternoon after work, and at night before going to sleep. Soon you will be able to achieve the same result without the ganzfield goggles. You can then reduce the number of repetitions of each phrase without losing the effect.

5. Activation

This aspect of ACT is virtually unknown in the West. Soviet psychologists, going a step further than their brothers and sisters in the West, have realized that relaxation, for all its benefits, can sometimes hamper performance. Activation (energizing the body and mind), designed to stimulate the sympathetic nervous system, thereby inducing the production of adrenaline in the bloodstream, is geared to induce such classic characteristics of the state of optimal functioning as dryness in the mouth, faster heartbeat, fast and shallow breathing, sensations of coolness and lightness in the body, and mental alertness.

Activation will counter drowsiness, mental sloth, lethargy, exhaustion, and depression, and fill you with new energy and enthusiasm.

During the first two weeks, activation should be used *after* immersion in ACS. Practice it during the day or early in the morning just after you wake up.

STIMULATING THE SYMPATHETIC NERVOUS SYSTEM

Here are the verbal and physical cues for self-inducing activation. (Don't forget to squeeze your left index finger and say the word *on* to get started.) Begin by saying:

"I've had *a good rest*" (repeat three times). Exhale on the first part of the phrase and inhale on the second. Try to couple the most meaningful part of the phrase (italics) with an inhalation, which is physiologically connected with tensing up the muscles.

"**I am breathing** ***deeper, inhaling energy***" (repeat twice). During the pauses between the phrases, visualize yourself inhaling a tiny cloud of white energy, which spreads throughout your entire body.

"**My body is** ***becoming lighter***" (repeat four times). Imagine that the white cloud of energy you inhale is a very light gas, like helium. Feel your body expanding like a balloon, becoming weightless, hovering above the bed.

"**My body is** ***becoming cooler***" (repeat four times). Imagine a fresh breeze blowing on your face. Feel the goose bumps appearing on your skin as you begin to shiver slightly. Coolness may be the most difficult physical effect to achieve; try conditioning yourself first with a cool shower.

"**My breathing is** ***getting faster***" (repeat four times). Be sure your breathing is fast and shallow, with a prolonged inhalation and a short exhalation, as you breathe through your mouth.

"**My mouth is** ***getting dry***" (repeat three times). Imagine that your mouth is becoming drier. Visualize yourself in a hot desert with no water in sight, becoming parched as the sun beats down on you.

"**Strength is** ***flowing into my body***" (repeat three times). Visualize a stream of vibrating energy pouring through your mouth into your body. It fills you with freshness and vigor. Feel yourself overflowing with this purifying energy; it now radiates from every pore of your body.

"**My muscles are** ***quivering with energy***" (repeat four times). Feel your muscles twitching in impatient anticipation for action. Strongly clench your fists and jaws several times.

"**My heart is *beating fast and strongly***" (repeat three times). Become aware of your pulse; feel it speeding up with every inhalation.

"**I am *vigorous and alert***" (repeat three times). Imagine strength, power, and a keen awareness of life expanding throughout your body.

"**I am *ready! Get up!***" (say once). At this point, count aloud to ten, starting slowly and escalating in rapid punctuation. When you reach ten, stand up.

Standing up, lower your head so your chin touches your chest. With your hands clasped behind your head, bring your elbows together in front of you. Inhaling slowly, try to raise your head while resisting this with your hands, and slowly rising on your tiptoes and opening your elbows, pulling your shoulders back. Hold this position for five seconds. Then, with an energetic exhalation, drop your shoulders and head.

THE CONTRAST SHOWER

An alternate physical method of activation, designed to charge you with energy for the whole day, is the contrast shower. The procedure is simple. In the morning, after you finish washing up, make the water considerably hotter and stand under the stream for about fifteen seconds. (Your body should be exposed to the heat twice as long as to the cold, because it takes longer for capillaries to dilate than to constrict.) Repeat the procedure at least three times, gradually increasing the difference between the temperatures of the water. Finish your contrast shower with a jet of cool water and then rub your body with a thick and rough bath towel until your skin turns red.

This exercise provides perfect "gymnastics" for your capillaries, making you more resistant to fatigue and even to the common cold. But take care: don't start your contrast showers with extremes of hot and cold water. Take about three weeks for the gradual change of temperatures, until eventually you finish your showers with ice-cold water.

6. Self-Control Exercises

USELESS-ROUTINE EXERCISE

Most of our actions pursue a certain practical purpose, from stretching a hand toward a glass of water to hammering a nail. But how about doing something without *any* practical purpose, simply to exercise and increase your willpower?

Set yourself some arbitrary, purposeless task once a day. It can be anything from putting a photograph face down in the morning and up at night, to placing a sock over your lamp at 8:00 P.M. The sillier or more useless it is, the better. A patient of mine used to place a left shoe in a cupboard every morning and touch her right ear at noon.

The major factor in the success of this exercise is choosing an action that can be done easily. Any strain must be avoided, because the goal is not to strengthen will but to sustain an action repeatedly during a prolonged period of time. In other words, do something extremely easy, but do it *regularly*.

We all perform certain actions regularly, out of habit: brush our teeth, get dressed, and so on. All these rituals have by now become unconscious. But consciously choosing your own rituals will serve to strengthen the pillars of your self-reliance.

THE SELF-CONTRACT

Make a contract with yourself. Choose four activities that you decide to perform every day, without exception. This method will establish an unshakable island of your free will, independent of any external or internal influences.

It's like making a bet with yourself—or, rather, making a bet with your Bruton drives (see Chapter 5). Put your pride at stake, the whole power of your very self against any distracting circumstances or excuses (fatigue, lack of time, bad weather). The self-contract will create an island of stability in your life, the area of your free will.

Take a look at the form that follows, and before filling it out, get acquainted with some basic rules:

1. Make your first two exercises purposeless, but the other two useful. The latter, however, must be easy: five push-ups in the morning, or learning one new word a day, for example. Remember, complexity serves as a perfect ground for failure.
2. Avoid ambiguity. Define your routine precisely. For example, don't just write "I will comb my dog every day"; write "I will comb my dog every day at 2:00 P.M., for five minutes."
3. Put limits on the duration of your exercises. Indicate a termination date; it shouldn't be longer than one or two weeks. Remember, nothing puts as much pressure on your resoluteness as infinity. This scary "forever" is somehow related to death.
4. Select the most meaningful person in your life and ask him or her to cosign your self-contract as witness. This will contribute external pressure to your resolution.
5. Maintain the chain of your self-contracts. Make a dozen copies of the self-contract sheet. Upon completion of your first self-contract, fill out a new one, calling for slightly more complex tasks. Try to avoid gaps between your self-contracts: the space

will serve as a perfect entry point for your Bruton to creep in. Continuity in keeping your resolutions will create a momentum of success.

ECHO-MAGNET

This exercise, developed by Dr. Vladimir Levy, the Soviet authority on self-control, is designed to ease the strain that results from the intense effort of working at something you consider important. The Echo-Magnet is a quick, effective method for easily commencing and sustaining any activity.

In general, there are two kinds of necessities: external and internal. The external necessity consists of all the things forced on us by life; it is expressed in the form of a "must": "I must do my homework," "I must be polite," "I must do the wash," and on and on. No wonder the satisfaction of external necessity is often connected with strain and displeasure. Conversely, internal necessity consists of all the things that make life livable, expressed in the form of "I want": "I want a new car," I want to get some rest," "I want to be happy." The tasks to satisfy these wants are approached with zest and pleasure.

By using the Echo-Magnet exercise, you can convert your "musts" into "wants."

The Echo-Magnet has three stages:

1. An emphatic command to yourself (stated with a lot of passion, pressure, drive).
2. Becoming truly empty and relaxed, ridding yourself of the slightest thought, until you achieve a state of total serenity.
3. Eliciting your ascending will.

SELF-CONTRACT

Forthwith and from this day forward I am willing and choosing to:

1. ____

____

2. ____

____

3. ____

____

4. ____

____

This is an irrevocable agreement I am making with myself.

Signature ______________________

Witness ______________________

Let's say you are sitting at the table, trying to start writing a report, staring at a pile of white paper. You feel a certain legitimate aversion to the task, which seems to be beyond your capabilities as well as interest.

Now it's time to start the Echo-Magnet exercise. Close your eyes and say, "I must write, I **must write**" (repeat eight times). Whisper it with ever-escalating fervor, until you reach a passionate crescendo, a demand. Then stop abruptly and let yourself flop back in your chair in a state of complete relaxation.

Now try to summon total indifference to the project, as you whisper, **"I don't want to write"** (repeat five times). Again build to passionate demand. Try to feel an emptiness, devoid of any trace of striving.

After about a minute, notice that something starts reverberating deep within you, and you will find yourself feeling: **"I want to write!"** (repeat it eight times).

Notice how saying the phrase gradually begets a feeling—a feeling of potency, of energy that restlessly wants to express itself in action. Once you start feeling this urge, grab your pen and start writing your report, riding along on the wave of this desire to write.

7. Personality Modification

Now that you have mastered ACT, you are finally ready to perform the powerful motivational exercises that you have been preparing for: Disidentification, Choosing Your Winning Mood, and Strengthening Desirable Co-Personalities. Through these exercises, you will learn how to rid yourself of your "loser" selves, how to pick and enter the optimum emotional state to carry you through any situation, and how to enhance and call forth the elements of your personality most likely to make you a winner or to ensure your maximum performance.

DISIDENTIFICATION

Disidentification is a process that allows you to distance yourself from your various co-personalities. It allows you to find your true center of identity (i.e., your consciousness), from which you can observe and regulate your various faculties.

That's all there is to it.

Find some quiet place and lie down on your back. After getting yourself in the auto-conditioning state, recite to yourself the following phrases. Repeat each phrase three times, visualizing it as fully and vividly as possible, exhaling on the italicized part of the phrase. (Make a two-breaths-long pause after each repetition.)

"I have possessions but *I am not my possessions*." Visualize yourself looking at all your possessions: house, car, clothes, and so on, and experience your separateness from all these material accoutrements.

"**I have a body but** ***I am not my body***." Visualize yourself stepping outside your body, looking at it from without, realizing that what you call "self" is different from your body.

"**I have thoughts but** ***I am not my thoughts***." Imagine your thoughts as butterflies, flying around your mental space. Become aware how easily they come and go, while your observing self remains the same.

"**I have emotions but** ***I am not my emotions***."

CREATING YOUR WINNING SELF

Peak performance, or the state of optimal functioning, as the Soviets call it, is largely a matter of mood or state of mind. Those who can choose their moods possess a definite edge in any competition. In the following exercise, "victory" is the emotion or mood that you will be trying to create within yourself. When you have an important task ahead of you, you can handle it much more successfully if you feel victorious. The mood that accompanies victory will engender self-confidence. However, you could choose "assertiveness" or "joyfulness" or whatever mood or emotion seems required to effectively deal with a situation.

After getting into ACS, visualize yourself lying on a deserted beach. You hear the pleasant sound of the waves; you feel the warm sun on your skin. Suddenly, you notice a narrow shaft of light emanating from the sun. It is slowly descending on you, reaching your forehead. You can feel the warmth-giving ray on your forehead. This beam is filled with vibrant, vivifying energy.

This energy becomes absorbed by your forehead, penetrating deeper, collecting inside, forming a ball of incandescent light. Now, clearly feel this ball of energy right inside your forehead. This ball of light represents your consciousness (i.e., your center of identity).

Now, identify yourself with the ball of light (call it "my center"). Picture your self located inside the ball of light, observing from it everything happening around you.

Recite the following phrase twice:

"I affirm my identity as *my center.* From my center *I can control my body."* Visualize your center shooting out beams of light, which reach all parts of your body (arms, legs, heart, etc.). These beams transmit the commands of your center to the various parts of your body.

Now say: "**From my center *I choose and control my thoughts***." Visualize your mental space as large as the room. At the top of the room is your center, a shining ball of light, from which you observe everything that is going on. The room is filled with butterflies—your thoughts. They are diverse and mobile, of different colors. Your center is able to shoot out a beam of light and direct it at any butterfly (i.e., any thought). The beam of light works like a leash; it can pull the captured butterfly closer to your center, so that you can examine the thought in greater detail. And you can keep the thought on your "leash of light" for as long as you want.

"**From my center *I choose and control my moods***." Visualize your moods being stored in the area of your solar plexus (we tend to store our emotions there). Imagine a chest of drawers, each of your moods set within its own drawer. The drawers are of different colors. Now, choose the colors of your emotions. What color is happiness for you? What about sadness? Irritability? Aggression? Label each with its own color.

You may wonder how all this can be used to choose and control your moods. The procedure is simple. Take victory, for example. Since you know that your thoughts cause your moods, first summon a victorious thought—one of those butterflies. The color of the butterfly should correspond to the color of the victory drawer in your solar plexus.

Let's say my color for victory is yellow. So I shoot out the beam of light from my center to my yellow victory butterfly. Here it is, right in front of my center, whispering the things I have "won at" in my life. The butterfly can start with those things I usually take for granted, such as "I earn a living. I am good at softball. I'm terrific at barbecuing."

After a few minutes of this "victory report," your yellow butterfly flutters down to your solar plexus and finds a yellow drawer, containing your victorious mood. The butterfly pulls the drawer open and . . . ah! A golden vapor rushes out from the drawer, spreading all over your mind and body, filling you with a victorious feeling. The moment the vapor pours out of the drawer, the yellow butterfly dissolves in it, symbolizing the fusion of thought with feeling.

The same method works for curtailing negative moods. You feel irritable and want to get rid of your irritability. Let's say that, for you, the color of irritability is gray. The first step is to summon your gray butterfly to your center and let it make an "irritability report" (i.e., all the reasons why you are irritable today).

After the report is over, the gray butterfly slides down

to your solar plexus and finds the gray drawer. But what is this? The drawer is already slightly open and the gray vapor of irritability is streaming outside, polluting your mental atmosphere. The gray butterfly squeezes itself into the open space and shuts the drawer from the inside, thereby locking itself inside as well.

PERSONALITY MODIFICATION

You can also use the disidentification technique to enhance and strengthen desirable areas of your personality. This procedure consists of three steps: minimizing your negative co-personalities, maximizing your positive ones, and action reinforcement.

1. DETECT AND MINIMIZE YOUR NEGATIVE IDENTIFICATIONS. What are your negative identities? Write down a list of your dominant negative co-personalities, those that rule your behavior the most often. They can be anything: loser, coward, victim, frustrated romantic, complainer, Jewish mama. Now give each one of them an image: your co-pers can look like a rock, an animal, a human being.

Now get into the auto-conditioning state (ACS) and recite to yourself:

"**I have a 'loser' co-pers but** ***I am not a loser***." Visualize your co-pers inside your head. See it melting down and evaporating with every exhalation.

Repeat the same procedure for every negative co-pers.

2. DETECT AND MAXIMIZE YOUR POSITIVE CO-PERSONALITIES. Take a look at your Target-Self list

(Chapter 2). Mark desirable qualities you would like to develop. Now translate them into co-personalities. Take courage, for example. The corresponding co-pers would be "Brave John" or "Brave Joan" (use your name, of course). Give it a shape. Recite the phrase: **"I am *'Brave John.'* "**

Visualize a situation that requires courage: an encounter with your boss, asking a friend for a favor, or fighting off your neighbor's dog. Visualize your brave co-pers as it fuses intimately with your center.

Become aware of the particular emotion that the image elicits. Stay with it for a while and give it color. Store it in one of the empty drawers in your solar plexus. Now you can call on it when you wish.

3. ACTION REINFORCEMENT. Create a situation in your life in which you can exercise your courage. Let it be something simple. If you experience fear of dealing with your boss or another colleague, start with the colleague. Try to choose a no-lose situation—for example, when you are clearly right in an argument. Recite to yourself the phrase, **"I am 'Brave John,' "** and summon the accompanying emotion. Now you are ready for confrontation!

After you win an argument, congratulate yourself for victory by being aware of your feelings of pride and self-respect. Remember that even a small victory makes you much stronger.

AFTERWORD

After reading this book, you may have the impression that each Soviet citizen is busy practicing various techniques of self-actualization. Nothing could be further from reality; the majority of the population has never even heard of self-actualization. The reason is simple: as much as the science of personality development is respected in the Soviet Union, there is a force more prevalent—ideology.

A totalitarian state built on Marxist dogma *has* to limit the degree of self-actualization of its citizens. Indeed, the inevitable outcome of personality development is a person capable of questioning the very foundations of the society and fighting for his individual convictions. This is exactly what the government doesn't want to happen. Highly evolved individuals, like Andrei Sakharov, run into a conflict with the Soviet system, threatening its very existence.

Samorazvitie, therefore, is a prerogative of a limited class of professionals whose performance is considered vital for the state. The rest of the population is kept "unenlightened" on these matters. In general, individuality is not encouraged in the USSR, for a simple reason—it's easier to govern a uniform collective of 280 million than an assembly of freethinkers.

The process of standardization begins early in life. The moment toddlers take their first steps, they find themselves members of Octabryonok (named for the month in which the Communists first came to power), a national organization designed to imbue in them Soviet society's standards and beliefs. The same functions are carried on by all the organizations that await the growing citizen—Young Pioneers, Comsomol (Communist Youth Union), and, finally, the Communist Party.

Hence come differences in the mentality of the Soviet man and woman, differences that somehow are ignored by Westerners misled by the dubious maxim, "People are basically the same everywhere."

One of the basic values of Soviet society, which sets it apart from the democratic social order, is this: the collective interest comes before the interest of the individual. In fact, a separate individual is viewed as something incomplete—the only "real person" is the collective. The ability to sacrifice oneself and others is one of the crucial traits of the Soviet citizen. Time and again, I was told that the value of individual life is measured by its importance to the collective. Your life does not belong to you; it's the property of your motherland. To give your life to your country is the highest human achievement possible. During World War II, the press glorified those citizens who threw themselves under enemy tanks with grenades in their hands.

The theoretical foundation of the general disregard for individual life in the USSR can be found in Karl Marx's famous dictum: "Society consists not of individuals but of the relations in which these individuals exist to each other." For example, two individuals in a factory exist in the social relation of "director—worker." It doesn't matter if the director's name is Ivanov and the worker's name Petrov. If Ivanov were to die tomorrow, his position would be taken by, say, Koslov, and the whole mechanism of social relation would continue to function as smoothly as before.

One sure way to make individuals feel an inseparable part of the whole is to strip them of their privacy. It is significant that there is no word for "privacy" in the Russian language. In Russia, everybody minds your business. Neighbors feel it's their duty to participate in the upbringing of your children. Familiarity is omnipresent: "How much is your rent, salary, dress?" There is no place to hide from the piercing curiosity of your neighbor; everyone's life *must* be an open book. In fact, complete openness is considered an attribute of an honest citizen; only the guilty one, it is thought, has any need for secrecy.

The Soviets seem to be more communal creatures than their American counterparts; they feel bored and anxious finding themselves alone, without the company of many friends. People spend tremendous amounts of time with one another, actively exchanging ideas, gossip, rumors. (In a country where the news is a monopoly of the state, gossip serves an important role in the dissemination of information.)

While on the surface Mikhail Gorbachev's reforms appear truly democratic, his celebrated "liberalization" of

Soviet society originates mostly from practical necessity, rather than from a true desire to change the system. Almost every day *Pravda,* with unheard-of candor, carries stories of high-ranking Soviet officials dismissed and prosecuted for bribery. Sound democratic? Well, it's not. The officials prosecuted for bribery, like the First Secretary of Kazakhstan, fell prey not to Gorbachev's *democratization* of society, but rather to his *optimization* of society. In other words, a corrupt bureaucrat inevitably is inefficient, and efficiency is the true goal of the *glasnost* campaign.

Gorbachev learned well from his predecessors that an economy based on slavery simply doesn't work. As was well known in ancient times, slaves are usually non-productive; they tend to be lazy, doing as little as possible, while stealing as much as they can from their masters. This has been the situation in the Soviet workplace for the last seventy years. The essence of Gorbachev's reforms can be boiled down to a simple goal: make lazy rascals work harder and see that they steal less.

The fact that he is attempting to accomplish this through reforms that smack of democratization and the encouragement, however limited, of a certain amount of private enterprise suggests that Gorbachev and other Soviet leaders are slowly coming to realize that the Russian people need to study and adopt the more effective of Western techniques in order to successfully compete against the Americans. That is why it is so critical for those here in the West to study the strengths of the Soviet system in order to successfully compete against the Russian edge.

BIBLIOGRAPHY

Aristotle, *Ethics*. New York: Everyman's Library, 1963.

Charles Darwin, *On the Origin of Species*. Cambridge, Mass.: Harvard University Press, 1975.

V. Davidov, *Psychological Conditions of the Origin of the Ideal Acts. Soviet Psychology,* May 19, 1980.

Christine Edwards, *The Stanislavsky Heritage.* New York: University Press, 1965.

Albert Einstein, *The World As I See It.* New York: The Wisdom Library, 1949.

Marilyn Ferguson, *The Aquarian Conspiracy.* Los Angeles: J. P. Tarcher, Inc., 1980.

L. Geller, "The Failure of Self-Actualization Theory." *Journal of Humanistic Psychology* 22(2): 56–73.

N. M. Gorchakov, *Stanislavsky Directs.* New York: Funk and Wagnalls, 1954.

Ronald Hingley, *The Russian Mind.* New York: Scribners, 1987.

William James, *Essays in Radical Empiricism.* Cambridge, Mass.: Harvard University Press, 1976.

Alex Kosulin, "The Concept of Activity in Soviet Psychology." *American Psychologist,* March 1986.

S. M. Kovalev, *Dialectic Materialism.* Moscow: Politicheskaya, 1972.

A. H. Leontyev, *Activity, Consciousness, Personality.* Moscow: Nauka, 1975.

A. H. Leontyev, *Problems of the Development of the Mind*. Moscow: Nauka, 1981.

Vladimir Levy, *The Art of Being Yourself.* Kemerovskoe Knizhnoye Izdatlstvo, Kemeroro, 1978.

Abraham Maslow, *Towards a Psychology of Being.* New York: Van Nostrand, 1962.

F. Mikhailov, *The Riddle of the Self.* Moscow: Progress, 1980.

V. P. Nekrasov, *Psychoregulation in Preparation of Athletes.* Moscow: Fiskeultra i Sport, 1985.

Friedrich Nietzsche, *The Gay Science.* New York: Vintage, 1974.

Friedrich Nietzsche, *Beyond Good and Evil.* New York: Vintage, 1983.

A. V. Petrovsky, *The History of Soviet Psychology.* Moscow: Prosvesheniye, 1967.

Plato, *Republic,* VII.

Levy Rahmani, *Soviet Psychology.* New York: International Univerity Press, Inc., 1937.

L. E. Ruvinsky, *Self-Development of Feeling, Intellect and Will.* Moscow: Znanie Publishing, 1983.

David K. Shipler, *Russia.* New York: Ballantine Books, 1983.

Hedrick Smith, *The Russians.* New York: Ballantine Books, 1983.

N. Talizina, *The Psychology of Learning.* Moscow: Progress, 1981.

A. I. Titarenko, *Marxist Ethnics.* Moscow: Politicheskaya, 1985.

Lev Vigotsky, *Consciousness as a Problem of Psychology of Behavior.* Leningrad: Znamya, 1925.

Voprosi Psychologii magazine, 1968, #2 (Russian edition).

Kenneth Walker, *A Study of Gurgieff's Teaching.* London: Jonathan Cape, 1980.